C0-DKN-292

by Carl Rakosi

Two Poems (1933)
Selected Poems (1941)
Amulet (1967)
Ere-Voice (1971)

Ex Cranium, Night / Carl Rakosi

1975
BLACK SPARROW PRESS
LOS ANGELES

EX CRANIUM, NIGHT. Copyright © 1975 by Callman Rawley.
All rights reserved. Printed in the United States of America. No
part of this book may be used or reproduced in any manner what-
soever without written permission except in the case of brief
quotations embodied in critical articles and reviews. For informa-
tion address Black Sparrow Press, P.O. Box 25603, Los Angeles, Ca,
90025.

Thanks are due the editors for previous publication of some of
these pieces in *Arts In Society, Big Sky, Chelsea, Chicago Lazarus,
Choice, Heartland II, Ironwood, Jargon 66, The Nation, New Di-
rections 25, 28 and 31, New Letters, North Country Anvil, North
Stone Review, One, Journal of the Otto Rank Society, Pembroke
Magazine, Unmuzzled Ox,* and to the following British and Aus-
tralian magazines and their editors, *Books, Grosseteste Review,
European Judaism, Iron Magazine, Prospice and Quadrant.* This
book owes a great deal to Yaddo and to Temple Israel in Minne-
apolis for the quiet and the atmosphere required to write a good
part of it.

LIBRARY OF CONGRESS CATALOGING IN PUBLICATION DATA

Rakosi, Carl, 1903-
    Ex cranium, night.

    I. Title.
PS3535.A415E9   811'.5'2   75-22242
ISBN 0-87685-238-X
ISBN 0-87685-237-1 pbk.

PS
3535
A415
E9

With love

to Leah

George   Leanna   Barbara

Jennifer   Julie   Joanna   Miriam

190736

TABLE OF CONTENTS

THE POET

EX CRANIUM, NIGHT

INSTRUCTIONS TO THE PLAYER

Cellist,
        easy on that bow.
Not too much weeping.

Remember that the soul
                is easily agitated
and has a terror of shapelessness.
It will venture out
           but only to a doe's eye.

Let the sound out
         inner *misterioso*
but from a distance
           like the forest at night.

And do not forget
         the pause between.
That is the sweetest
and has the nature of infinity.

THE GLASS OF MADEIRA

Madeira,
       you have put me
into a null state.
         Now I know
what the Eskimo meant
           when he said,
"The weather is our master."

I know, you want me
           in a kind of interval
or heavy water.
          Another glass
and I'll be your placebo.

Well, I feel no pain.
           I'll rest awhile
in this ancient limbic system.
If I sit here long enough,
            I may figure out
the gravitational pull
         of words:
viz., "The sea is old
         but the earth is older."

The vine from which you came
             was brought from Cyprus
by the Portuguese
         to the island of Madeira
where the green canary abounds
and sixhundredninetyfive species of beetles.
The coast is rocky
         and the sea unquiet,
hence there are few algae.
The rock is basalt
         of volcanic origin,
dark and hard.
There are few meadows and pastures.
The cattle feed on the mountains
and on the lower slopes
          are a few towns.

14

This is said
            to reassure
men of facts
            dragging an ass.

Good Madeira,
            let me lie in your glass
in the mellow quality
            of latency.
Do not unlock us.
            The cubic light
of a small planet
            left its source
at the time of Prospero,
            iron-red,
and entered here.

            What time is this?
the axis of the earth inclines,
            the fish swims to the hook,
the old man plants
            a plum tree for his granddaughter.

Profound Madeira,
            let me get some of this pressure
off my bladder.
            I'm stoned.
I don't know my backbone
            from a tuning fork.
Don't anybody
            bump my arm
or try to stop me.

Undefinably deep and strange
            is this lighted enclave,
this underwater amber,
like the words of a philosopher
            with a taste for style:
"There is mustard seed
            in the shape of the earth.
But it doesn't matter."

In this condition

15

it is easy to be deceived.
The last words
                of Beethoven on his death bed
after four operations, "Too late! Too late!"
also looked profound
                        until the reference was traced
to a shipment of his favorite Rhine wine.

Verily, I slobber over.
It wouldn't surprise me
                        if four mink
dashed across this scene,
                        pulling an orange crate.
I wouldn't bat an eye.

What's the matter?
Don't we peasants
                deserve to be entertained?

I'm not going to budge
                from this love seat
until Leah calls.

ISRAEL

I hear the voice
         of David and Bathsheba
and the judgment
           on the continual backslidings of the Kings of Israel.
I have stumbled on the ancient voice of honesty
and tremble
        at the voice of my people.

SERVICES

There was a man in the land of Uz.

Who's that at my coattails?
A pale cocksman.

Hush!
The rabbi walks in thought
                          as in an ordained measure
to the Ark
          and slowly opens its great doors.
The congregation rises
                 and faces the six torahs
and the covenant,
            and all beyond.
The Ark glows.
               Hear, O Israel!

The rabbi stands before the light
inside, alone, and prays.
It is a modest prayer
for the responsibilities of his office.
The congregation is silent.

I too pray:
Let Leah my wife be recompensed for her sweet smile
and our many years of companionship,
and not stick me when she cuts my hair.
And let her stay at my side at large gatherings.
And let my son George and his wife Leanna
and my daughter Barbara be close,
and let their children, Jennifer, Julie and Joanna
be my sheep
             and I their old shepherd.
Let them remain as they are.

And let not my white hair frighten me.

The tiger leaps,
the baboon cries,
Pity, pity.

The rabbi prays.

There was a man in the land of Uz.

I, son of Leopold and Flora,
also pray:
I pray for meaning.
I pray for the physical,
for my soul needs no suppliant.
I pray for man.

And may a special providence look out
for those who feel deeply.

AIE!

There's the greenwood fern
and the open woods
and the smell of hay
and the eye of a frog
and a fern signature
left in a coal

and there is fern by analogy,
a most ancient weed.

CENOZOIC TIME

A man looks
            at a rock.
The rock sits.
                Rock and man.
The rock is.
            What is being?

He has sensed his nature,
idea as idea,
and trembles
before the insoluble art.

RIDDLE

In the dead of night
the caribou slept.

The possibility of not knowing
what you are
had not yet been conceived.

It is the original forest.
There is peace.

The wolf has eaten.
He goes into a long howl
to give his location.

If the hunter does not find him,
he'll live seven years.

A box is a box.
Integrity has been defined.

LITTLE OBSERVATIONS AT YADDO

Dark woods.
           Deep inside,
a clearing
       with light
as in a bowl /
          because
of the darkness
         lovely.

Further on
        a gorge
and far down
         at the bottom
a tiny stream /
         grace issues
from the eye.
        As if framed.

Small boys
       fishing under a sign:
NO ONE ALLOWED BEYOND THIS GATE.
Eye me:
      wary.
The first to get a nibble.
Protected by a special providence
or else the bass love them.

Fish die.
       Without compunction.
Strange!
       The soundless order.
Not one
      of the noble
biosphere,
       the bleeders.
All skeletal.
       The eyes
tell nothing.
       That must be it!
no soul there.

       Enters humanity
through my eyes.

Darkness
       on the water.
Dense green
         moss below.
Thick branches
         overhanging
Whittier's bare
       foot boy.
No, he's too healthy.

Behind me
      a hawthorn bush.
Hawthorn! a cloying
         word
even to Coleridge
but not to middle English.

No one here
       but my eyes.
A long breath.
         Torpor.
Liquifies.
      Limbs vibrate,
tingle ⁄
      the true physical.

Lakes being
      timeless,
yet in time.
       I have lost
my identity.
       The light
makes me
      invent nymphs . . .
and hang on
      exclamation marks . . .
and call to them
      and they call back.

Must be

                    how myths arose,
        the distant
                        luminous ones,
        motionless
                    as in eternity.

HOW TO BE WITH A ROCK

The explicit ends here.
$\qquad\qquad$ Outer is inner.
It is all manifest.
$\qquad\qquad\qquad$ Its character is durity.
There lies its charisma.

By nature it is Pangaea.
$\qquad\qquad\qquad\qquad$ It has its own face
and its own tomb,
$\qquad\qquad\qquad$ the way it stands
unmoved by destiny,
$\qquad\qquad\qquad\qquad$ a model for the mind.
We can only be spectators.
$\qquad\qquad\qquad\qquad$ All is day within.

"Go to the village," I tell my wife,
"and bring back a chicken,
$\qquad\qquad\qquad\qquad$ an onion, a goose
and an apple
$\qquad\qquad$ and we'll lie here
and repopulate this Siberia."

It is in Genesis.
A strange god,
$\qquad\qquad$ all torso
and without invention or audacity.

It can be accused of both plutonism
and the obvious.
$\qquad\qquad\qquad$ The closest human thing to it
is the novocained tooth
$\qquad\qquad\qquad\qquad$ its Medusa hair now fossilized.

It can be bequeathed to one's heirs
with the assurance that it will not depreciate
or be found irrelevant.

TESTING ON STEEL AND GLASS

"If you open the brain,
                    from whence sprang Solomon and Aristotle,
and separate the lips
                    in the fissure of Sylvius,
a triangle of cortex will appear.   This is the Island of Reil."

Well put, anatomist.
                    We are all careful, men of earth:
a blind man can sense a post.

Thus Newton pondered on falling apples
and a Mixtec carved a humanist in jaguar bone.

"How happy I was,"
                    wrote the scientist after a long illness,
"when once again
                    I had something to investigate."

GROUND BREAKING

If it takes almost a million years
                              for light from Andromeda
to reach a learned society

and stars sometimes explode
                              on the astronomer's time scale

and in another hundred million years
                              we shall be able to see
Maffei I,
          described as "a nearby island universe,"

then there is passion
                in the lightness of a feather,
man can hear
            his arteries hardening,
and the realist must pass
                     first through the eye of abstraction.

Yet they say it is so.

THE ADVENTURES OF VARESE

By ordinary wind
          and percussion instruments
and a granite will
          we broke out of the romantic
gravitational field.
          The idea
was to reach *sui generis*,
          a state of random mass
above sensitivity.

Then cymbals crashed
          and America cowered . . .
girders ground
          against each other . . .
but it was spared,
          and massive bulkheads rammed and groaned.
Inevitable, once heard.

The smaller sounds drifted aimlessly
          like fish
and nudged . . .
          creaking winches,
ratchets,
senseless clap   clap   clap
then darted from the shark.

But after that we heard cowbells
and knew we were not far from a meadow
and had our legs
          and smell yet
and could still remember.

A jazz trombone.

Was that memory
          or something out there
putting on a black face
          and blowing "Haw Haw"?
We were afraid.

I think there was a trumpet too
but it was brief,
                        a mere scarf.
And a triangle,
                        very delicate.

Again we heard a crash like before Genesis
of portent without soul,
                        and America cringed,
expecting to be shattered.
                        And from far off, screaming,
a fire siren bore down on us
                        on a stage street,
a fiasco.

        Then a tugboat plying space was heard.
Then nothing.
                W e waited,
despondent, wrung out.

Suddenly we heard a flute playing,
                        aloft, lovely,
a plutonium I,
                sweet and limpid,
and knew we were still in romantic gravity.
But girders ground against each other
and America wept.

THE MAD AGE

Icon and
           iconoclasm
both pursued.
               Hoopla!

At the inner ear:
                 liquid patter
of a soft mallet,
                  cymbalom
running pianissimo,
                    fruit tones
out of wood.

THE INDOMITABLE

copulate
          < *copulare:*
to join,
       to couple;
says nothing
         of lust,
the iron master,
           sweaty,
breathless,
       fierce.

NUCLEAR ODE

We shall all lie in the sun
                    and bask.

You too, hunter.
There shall be no more loners,
                    do you hear?

ANIMA

When she was two, she told herself, "I'm not bad."

How did she learn so early that the voice comes with its own stage and that there were two of her, one to help the other? Somewhere along the way she must have discovered that she was observing and at the same time talking to her mother and that if she could do that, she could also talk to herself and observe herself doing it.

Young children are playing mother and child. The "mother" issues fierce / irrational commands and beats horrendous punishments down on the hapless heads. They submit, wordless. None of them was willing to play the child. Only the youngest could be bullied into it.

Do not these exorcising games contain the enigmatic pathos and symbolism of art?

When she was sixteen, she was in a trance-like polarity . . . full, voluptuous lips against a far-away look in her eyes, pure hazel. Voluptas was in the inner city but the eyes were forbidden to show it. They had fled to the north to remain chaste and cool and to escape public disaster, for it must never be glimpsed that she had been surprised and taken, or that fighting had been going on. The transiency and inaccessibility of that loveliness was unbearably moving.

Two years later the eyes had become clear and self-confident and held one firmly, the teeth had become larger, the face strong. A peasant had moved in.

Poignancy

On a bus: man in his fifties, a spare, closed face, reading *Time*. When he moves his arm, French cuffs protrude from his beige stormcoat. You know by their pure light blue that this shirt has been laundered like fine lace by his wife, using only distilled water, ironing and folding it patiently, as meticulous as if she were wearing a surgical mask. She has a closed face too. Her soul, in fact, is in this shirt, for in bed she is inert, and there is no other way to get close to her.

34

XANADU

"PURSUANT TO THE ROCKS,
THORNS."

(words from a dream)

I instantly knew that these words were intended to tell me something which I should know. Their heavy stress indicated that they were meant to be mouthed. The dream part had disappeared like an early Greek hero of obscure origin except for a residue in my mind of a night of turbulence and alarums. And I could remember, too, whether in the dream or afterwards is dim now, that I knew by a fleeting image of deserted streets and dust and paper flying around that the turbulent action, swelling and heaving, had come to an end the way a huge wave subsides into ordinary water lapping along the shore.

I felt as if I had been through a fever. I had the distinct impression that the whole human race had come out of the ocean before my eyes and that a great drama of passion had just been enacted. But the image disappeared quickly. I remained certain, however, that this is the way it had happened and that for a moment I had glimpsed the event.

"Pursuant to the rocks, thorns," the words had been spoken in my head, distinct but not loud, and had the presence of a stone engraving. From that I gathered that they had something to do with the stern, underlying order of things and that they were exact and absolute and must not be changed in any way. I could make nothing but poetic sense out of them, yet in some way they were intended to guide me.

That is how I came to know how God spoke to Moses.

"Let Malchia bless with the Bat,
Let Rebecca rejoice with Lynx."

These lines written by Christopher Smart in madness I often hear, responding to them like a harpstring, though I am not mad.

But *bless* with a bat? *Rejoice* with a lynx? I break into a cold sweat at this awful reordering of nature.

And *Bat* capitalized! What dark irrational force is meant by that?

Yet I have been in the same presence, alone at night in the forest, and I am spellbound in the deepest part of my unconscious where there is no perception of purpose in the universe, by the alliance of Smart with these dark forces.

THE DEPRESSION DREAM

8:20 a.m.

*The Competitive
Examination
(no notice posted)*

*how hard
to move!*

Massive stone.
A public gray building.
Shadowy applicants
mill around
slowly   slowly
he among them
no one speaks
or looks

*8:30 a.m.
City Clerk's window
lights up*

The nameless plodders,
the inner downtrodden
—O patient ones!
in the shadow
of the labor market:
figures smudged in gray
charcoal like men
on a bread line,
I as drab and sodden as the others.

*the dread
must not be
divulged*

It was not possible to say
whether the hysteria I felt
was in me or in that dense time
when I was starting out as a young man,
the necessity to make a living
the cement shaft of my backbone.

*standing
at the window*

A blotted word was not
so indistinct as he.
The air
mucous and dispirited.

*told: "Too late!"
worms way
into line
for next exam*

How hard it was to tell
time from foreboding,
they were both so heavy and inert.

*barely moves
reaches window
waits patiently*

*Afraid:
his chance
blown!*

I recognized
                    the grave masque:
Civil Servant In His Cubicle,
twelve paces from his desk
to the public window;
answer question;

hand out form;
peruse
       in the slow measure
of a document
          and crawl
twelve paces back.
How can I describe
who I was there?

tries to catch
Clerk's eye

The remote figure is oblivious,
waits on others.
Anger then
        (like water
warming up
      and starting to stir
over a burner)
        threw a javelin
from the eye.

mouth open
straining to shout
mouth still open

"Now look here!
I demand! . . ."
no sound

Late afternoon,
closing time /

Five mules of weight.

tugs and heaves:

"I must!"

the Clerk then
disappears
altogether,
like an electric
current
suddenly dead

and I awoke,
its dim buzzing still in me.

What is the point?

Next time I'm lying on my back,
my sinuses clogging up
and far inside my head as in a swelling
one nerve vibrates,
unable to transmit its impulse,
I must remember to turn over.
I'd like another chance.
Just once I'd like to be
          able to make it
in this chicken-shit theater.
But if I'm always going to be

afloat on a becalmed sea
like the ancient mariner,
                    to hell with it.
I'll stick to the earth's atmosphere
where it is "wondrous clear and exhilarating"
and I can take my steel out
                    and make me visible.

TWICE NOW IN DREAMS

Twice now in dreams I am walking and as I turn a corner, I bump into this angry dwarf. Both times he is with two men of normal height, jabbering away in Spanish, a language I do not understand. In the first dream he shot them a quick look to see if they would back him up if he started a fight, but the incident blew over and the three men disintegrated as suddenly as magician's smoke. The second time we bumped, I apologized for my awkwardness with an elegant flourish of my right hand, noting in my dream, from a distance, how rich my metaphors were. At the same time, I was aware dimly that something inexorable was about to be acted out. Sure enough, my apology had no effect on the dwarf. His cheeks puffed up like a bullfrog's, blazing red with rage, and taking advantage of my contrite mood, he stepped up on my shoes and ground his heels into them. With that the second dream ended.

Who was this preposterous little scrapper and why did he have it in for me? And what was the heavy import I sensed? That they were speaking Spanish had something to do with it, but no one close to me was native to Spanish. I was stumped and would have given up but the malevolence of the dwarf would not let me, and for some inexplicable reason the head of Borges kept appearing like a head in a doorway. After a while I noticed that it always followed the dwarf and I concluded that there must be some connection.

I had met Borges in 1970 at the University of Wisconsin. L. S. Dembo had just finished interviewing him for *Contemporary Literature* and was putting his tape machine away. The others were scurrying around for their coats, getting ready for the Spanish Department's big dinner for him. Borges was sitting on the edge of a couch, motionless, the body slumped. He looked alone and bleak, the basic lot of blindness. Di Giovanni, his translator, took me by the arm and walked me over to him and introduced me, saying something about me in Spanish so that Mrs. Borges would also understand. Instantly, Borges' face lit up and the nimble mind was back at attention at its station, lambent anima. He spoke English in a melodious voice, affectionate and low-keyed, as with an old friend, interested in everything I had to say, and I responded eagerly in instant bond as if I were resuming a conversation with him where I had left off years ago. And so as friends do, I took him gently by the lapel, pulling him towards me, and carried along, found myself starting off on a teasing note.

"You complain about your memory, Borges," (I had heard that in Argentina friends address each other by their last names) "but I've just heard you. It's inexhaustible!"

He looked doubtful.

"I can't remember dates any more."

Was this a slight put-on?

More words. Then the scurrying voices around us, all talking at once, stopped. The room was empty. Even di Giovanni and Mrs. Borges had disappeared. Gone to get the cars. Or maybe to give Borges the opportunity to be alone with a writer and to escape briefly themselves from their chores.

I had been elected to be his escort. So arm in arm, in close step, the only way you can walk and at the same time talk with a blind man, we went down a long hall, in and out of an elevator, down the stairs and out into the street. The sudden intimacy went to my head and I felt myself in a charmed circle, my voice speaking.

"You know, Borges, your blindness may have been a blessing to you. It protected you against distractions."

No, distraction was never a problem for him. But it might have forced him to live more in his imagination.

He was interested in why I had stopped writing for so long.

"It was my misfortune to fall in love with social work."

"Nothing was lost then. I too stopped writing once, for a whole year. I had nothing to say."

As we got to the car, he asked which way it was facing so that he would know which way to sit. In the restaurant I read the menu to him, our heads together. What did I recommend? The question was earnest. Where was his knife? I put it into his hand. His napkin? His helplessness drew me to him, consummating. Di Giovanni walked over and whispered into my ear, "I think he prefers to be with you, Carl."

Di Giovanni is a busy, somewhat nervous person. He knew me only as someone associated with Objectivism, yet called me affectionately by my first name. I don't know

43

whether it was the liquor or the atmosphere but I felt a gush of emotion and I remember thinking, Is the great friendliness I feel locked up in me finally visible in my face for all men to see? And I wept inwardly.

"Let me tell you an anecdote," said Borges, and he told two, every detail clear and perfectly in place. They were anecdotes of cruelty. His only interest was in the story. The inhumanity was just its cement, and he was only mildly interested in whether people in real life tended to be cruel. He hoped not.

When he learned that I was Hungarian, he asked whether I would say something in that language. He'd like to hear how it sounds. I said a few words but was ashamed to admit that I could no longer speak it. He looked disappointed. He had expected a poem.

Young Argentine writers try desperately to be contemporary, he said. Forget all that, he tells them; you *are* contemporary, no matter what you write. His opinion of South American universities was low. He teaches English at the University of Buenos Aires but that couldn't be taken seriously now, could it? Right now he's teaching Anglo-Saxon because he wants to learn it himself. It's only interesting to teach something if you're learning it at the same time. And off he went into an Anglo-Saxon poem, a whole army of ringing iron sounds marching out erect, drums rolling. William Ellery Leonard, the old bard who had taught Anglo-Saxon at Wisconsin, was a tin-eared piker by comparison.

Then with mock pride he referred to his Northumbrian grandmother and to the great English books in his father's library, the same classics that had moved me as a boy. Evidently he had learned his flawless English there, softer in sound and more elegant than ours, with just a suggestion of the liquid gentleness I think I have sometimes heard in Spanish.

He mentioned Frost with admiration. I countered with Cummings. Like a shot he launched joyfully into a Cummings poem. Borges' personal stamp was all over it.

"Imagine condemning a writer for having been influenced," he said, referring to an adverse review he had once read of Cummings.

"The thing about Cummings was his complete trust in his feelings," I said.

"Of course" (as if this went without saying for any

44

writer), "but I wonder how he is regarded today."

Was he thinking that such spontaneity no longer had a place with this generation?

"He's very popular with students."

He looked puzzled.

Recalling his low opinion of South American culture, I asked him whether he knew that recent South American poetry had influenced some of our poets. This drew a blank. He could find no possible explanation for such a thing.

"Maybe it's the appeal of passion to inhibited natures," I said, putting a note of fun into my voice. But he took it straight. He couldn't account for the influence. It simply didn't register in his mind.

The time had come to leave for his big lecture to the Spanish faculty. Everybody was feeling high. Mrs. Borges was standing by the men's room and pointing with her eyes.

"Please," she said to me, the only words she knew in English.

I took him inside and as we stood at the urinals, I asked, a bit apprehensively, if he would like me to send him my last book. Did he have some way to read it?

"Yes, yes!" (still fingering himself at the stall). His voice was eager: "Take down my name, Jorge Luis Borges," and he spelled it out carefully letter by letter. "Biblioteca National."

He seemed to have no sense whatever of his fame.

On the way out I asked him if his lecture was going to be in Spanish. From the expression on his face I knew at once that I had put him into an awkward position. He hesitated. He hadn't decided, he said. The Spanish faculty hadn't told him what language to use. Courtesy was struggling with responsibility in his mind. Then he made a decision and his face lit up.

"I'll speak in English. For you!"

It was obvious that they were expecting him to speak in Spanish and so I couldn't accept, but I had the feeling that he would have preferred English.

The night was clear and starry. He was in a gay mood.

"Ah, Spanish. Not much of a language, eh? Bu English . . ." and he gently caricatured a British accent but in the tone of one who felt there was honor in having that in your heritage . . . "there's a language, what? Northumberland,

45

you know, North of England. Proud to be from there. Ha! Ha!"

We were standing outside waiting for the car to take him to his lecture. Suddenly he broke into a German poem. The accent, the vernacular sound of the German, the inner music, were impeccable. In the lovely evening it flowed as if there were some universal mind which writes all poetry, in whose blithe spirit lay the only true camaraderie. He looked at me as if recalling a transfigured moment out of our past. Alas, I had not been there. I did not know the poem, but not a muscle moved in me for fear of breaking the spell.

The cars were pulling up now. It was time to go. I felt reluctant to part. A car drove up for him. The door was open. It could no longer be put off. We embraced and parted.

This was the man then to whom my dream had some connection. But how could he be the dwarf? Impossible. Di Giovanni couldn't be considered either. He hadn't done anything but introduce me. Nowhere could I see any sign of the identity of that vile dwarf. Yet I could not give up. There had to be a connection. Round and around I went. Occasionally I sensed that the answer was near.

Then as if someone in the background who had been slightly amused at so much determination finally relented, I heard, as in a symbol, the words, "Well, all right, if you're going to be *that* persistent . . . ." At that moment the answer flashed on me: *I* was the dwarf!

It was the way I saw myself, possibly by comparison to Borges' world reputation, which like a great noumenon had straddled the announcement: THE DEPARTMENT OF SPANISH AND PORTUGUESE OF THE UNIVERSITY OF WISCONSIN ANNOUNCES THE VISIT AND PUBLIC LECTURE OF JORGE LUIS BORGES, RENOWNED ARGENTINE SHORT STORY WRITER, POET AND CRITIC.

How ineluctably such comparisons drag the gut out of a man. The odious disparity had contracted me into that repulsive dwarf. It was now clear why I had been so angry and pugnacious. But my determination and nerve were only paper tigers, for in the dream the dwarf had stolen a quick glance at his companions to see if they would stand by him if the fighting started.

No wonder the little bugger couldn't be appeased despite the elegant flourish of my right hand and the richness of my apology. The person he had bumped into was not I but

46

Borges! Borges was now unmistakably recognizable in that flourish and that richness of language. I had caricatured a stereotype of the South American writer of an earlier generation.

Often the protagonist in dreams is a mysterious figure but in this dream there was no mystery about why Borges had taken my place. Had I not thought when the living Borges and I parted, "I have a Borges in me. In fact, it is easier for me to be Borges than myself. I see more clearly who he is."?

So I can relax. Though I had made an angry dwarf stomp on Borges' foot, I had not demeaned him. The fact is, he would have treated me far more kindly than I had treated myself.

But then, innocence has left Xanadu.

NIGHT

The thing that sits self-conscious in the intellect and longs to be great is not the soul. The soul wants only a gentle planet.

It is not in our nature to live as if life came to an end. And if by chance we could, it would not seem worthwhile.

HOW GOES IT WITH TIME?

For H. S. Ephron

The auditors have sent me notice.
There is not enough left in my account
to piss with

but what there is
will cure vanity
and end metathesis

and make a cabbage of me:
all my value will be under ground.

If I could look at it
I would not.

In short, it is all that matters.
The agenbite of iron.
The rest can be learned.

Are God and man streaming in opposite directions?
. . . man towards the grand, the universal—mystical because
it is not attainable—and God, since He is already in possession
of that, towards the elementary particles of matter and the
bursting inexhaustability of a moment.
The forces are too powerful for love.
The poet has a sense of both vectors.

The question, What for? has an electric presence
unaffected by rational probing, a kind of eternal life, in part
inside our own nature. It is more peaceful than an answer and
does not seem to need one, it is so grand-scaled. Perhaps it is a
divine tool left in us, or the sign to consummation.
When it is asked, we know at once that it is our
question and that the thing that really matters is in it
somewhere, along with our missing scope.
It is so unaccountably deep and leads into such
strange places that the nature of God may be studied there.
But with what?

MEDITATION

All those stricken by cancer,
                            yet I still am!

Then a voice:
            "Be honest.
Who is there to thank?
Besides, you would turn God
                            into a man."

"Ironist, when I say
                the heart of man,
do you not know what I mean?
Do you not likewise overflow?

You do not know me.
                        Get out of the way!
My heart yearns for its referent."

The secular is long
                but not as long as paradox.
On this, meaning
                and divinity depend.

Eternity has a blank face in mathematics but its character stands revealed in the human will.

Thus began *ad infinitum* and the first philosopher: a man contemplating a rock.

If God were fictive, He would still be our noblest fiction.

AN AGELESS FACE

That gives the orbit.
The eyelids hang low
(low clearance):
dark and sad.
That's for utterance.

An undertaker left
his bags here.

All here.

Experience feels infinite, as if there were no reason why *it* should cease. Yet it does.

The same duality is in time and poetry.

Therein lies their enigma and strange power.

We write and poetry is sad because our aspirations are of a different order than reality and hence not attainable. People go about their business as if this order did not exist and mistakenly assume that their primal disappointment and anguish are occurring in the everyday world.

THE HISTORY OF MAN

That cry of agony
                    from a carious tooth:
the man from the age
                    of orogenies
has left his parameters
                    in us
and a memory of his ordeal.

Whatever my good fortune, a grave, archaic voice in me cries, "The matter is not so. If it were only this, it would not have been worthwhile."

Nor is the matter in misfortune, although I am closer to my self there.

It is, rather, in my own nature. There is something there I have not yet glimpsed for which I yearn. It trembles so, it is pathos, and is too irrational for words. It is appalling as the inchoate at the opening of Genesis, its pit, its foreverness. What deprivations I would endure to reach it! Nothing else matters, nothing, nothing.

The look ahead in time is shallow. It seems to have been designed only to make the present work. There's no philosophy in that.

It's the look backwards that leads into the eyes of philosophy, and from there to man's depth.

The response to Hamlet: Leakey, the British anthropologist, beholding for the first time the skull of Zinjanthropus, 1,500,000 years in his hand.

THE STREET

Like slag
      the face,
old,
one who knows he has been banished,
knows the place,
expects no sympathy or interest.

At seeing me
        the face
lit up at once
        and smiled,
expecting a smile:
           You're one of us!

What is the nature of *quintessence?*

The word comes from alchemy but there is nothing alchemical about the question. It is asked seriously and yearns for an answer, but since there is none, the question must be poetical.

Its sister word is *nature*, as when Aristotle writes, "A spirit in the body of the seed whose *nature* answereth in proportion to the element of the stars."

Ah, how lovely that is! I long to make my presence known to it. It is so physical, I could touch it with a finger tip.

I had been reading a passage from Nietzsche, gripped by its power: *O Mensch! Gib acht! Was spricht die tiefe Mitternacht!* when suddenly I noticed that the passage ended with an exclamation point, not a question mark, as I had at first read. I had naturally assumed that Nietzsche, the poet in love with deep questions, would end the passage the way I would have, with a question mark. I was startled to find the fire and brimstone of the moralist bearing down on me.

PROBLEMS OF THE AGED

"You look remarkably young."

I? The old mandrake root?

"The white hair
                    has not reached your genitals yet!

"What do you do all day?"

I plant radishes, you damn fool!

And hang around doctors' offices,
                                    medical hands on me,
waiting for the report.

And crack jokes:
                    "I don't deserve this.
I've been faithful to my wife!"

To whom can one turn?

"She was a great beauty in her youth
and came from a distinguished family."

What is the earthly point of that?

The unrelenting eyes spoke:
"You knew you were going to be old.
Why didn't you prepare for it?"

Well, I have had kindnesses.
                        But the inexorable!
That's only good
                    for making eyes compassionate.

So there's a scale
                    to the rest of me.
Who is there
                    to carry that burden?

And a dew drop
                    to collect my affinity
for earth.

Merde!

We realize the body's terrible import only when it is irreversibly sick!

Perhaps the curtain is drawn out of compassion.

Plants and animals: each has its own individual shape and set behavior in order to survive. But by what mystery are they also beautiful?

Who knows what the body means until it is sick? Then it is too late to be loved, and the meaning has entered the sickness itself, unnatural and tortured.

THE INCURABLE ILLNESS

I am ninety years old.
I don't think anymore.
                    It can't help me.

Who could look at me
                    lying here
and know what I was?

A woman sobbed in the passage.

Now the aged mother can no longer be loved. Her whole body has shrunk. The flesh hangs on her upper arms. The teeth have a brown stain and are loose and ratty. She keeps falling and bumping into things, and has to be chauffeured everywhere. And there is no end to the doctors, the expense, her pain.

No one now knows how to enter her situation. And who would want to? It is hard, in fact, for the daughter to look directly at her. She is afraid of what the mother will see in her eyes, that she has become tedious and that nothing she could say could ever be of interest any longer.

And so the daughter, who at first could not bear to see her mother aging, comes in time to wait for the end doggedly as in an iron cast without the grief and pathos she would feel if the mother were still the same person she knew as a young woman.

There is a kindly providence in this for her, but not for the mother.

AT THE GRAVESIDE

Yes, I was old.
My colon had become as thin
                           as the middle finger.
The joints had swollen
                      into clenched fists.
I had stones
           the size of clinkers.
Leonardo dissected me
                     and was astonished
that they looked like iron.

There was a time
               when I came to a place like this
and put on a special face too
                            and stood motionless,
thinking,
         "Only he can say,
'No more anxiety.
Never. Never. Never.' "

I had a way with words.

AT THE OPEN CASKET

We had the same mother,
                    the same father,
walked the same streets.
                    Often we were waylaid
on our way to school
                    and would scrap side by side.
Our underclothes
                    with the fresh smell of soap
used to lie
                    neatly folded
in the same drawer.

(Takes off his tie
                    and hands it to the undertaker)
"Put this on him.
                    He was always neat."

In the end is the man
                    of flesh.
He leaped into the grave
                    for that principle.

His habits,
                    too, were principles.
His voice as a man,
                    the warmth,
thick in phlegm
                    far back of the palate.

The eyes
          looking inward
a light entering
                    like a pin head
as a comic memory
                    came into his mind.
His bearing, modest;
he was taken for ordinary.

How loveable he appears
                    from this distance!

In the end is the man
                    of family.

I must look at him again.

The features are the same,
though less pinched, less nervous.
The color in his cheeks is fairly natural.
There's dignity the way he's stretched out.
Objective cancelled.
                    Out of work.
Lies as in a pause.
                    Very peaceful.
(I don't remember that!)

That's the undertaker's specialty.
The man's gone mad in physics,
                    I in metaphysics.

There is a grandeur and a poetry in a simple question like, "What are animals for?" which is not even conceivable in answers.

A strange coupling, implausible yet somehow belonging together: mountains at night, their mystery, and the image of Borges poring over ancient occult documents for the language of mystery.

With age the heart cries like a child and is afraid of being left alone.

I have the feeling that if I ever got close to beholding God, I would instantly become transfixed into a lifeless stick. Why then am I still secular?

The word *reverence* baffles me, for I have found nothing that I can honestly say I revere. Yet nothing touches me more deeply than that word. It has sent me a messenger in the slow, grave measures of music, and in the silences between.

Out of the way, wit, I yearn for long distances.

I shall not prevail. The heart is my negritude.

AMERICANA

The "Americana" poems in my last three books are a documentary at two levels . . . the thing being talked about, and its stereotype, plain and corny. For the one, the voice is straight, for the other, the stereotype, it is amused and ironic. In this impossible combination I touch base from time to time and hear the voice of American humor, guffawing with a straight face, for the two have become so commixed that it's hard to say which is which. But this too is as American as,

> "Where the road forks at the red barn
> and the oak tree has a knot hole
> on its north side . . ."
>   ("Americana V," *Amulet*)

and I would not want to change one freckle on its homely face. All I have tried to do is put them into such essential phrasing that it reveals the irony of their situation. Some "Americana," however, like IV and V in *Amulet* had a mind of their own and insisted on going their own somber way.

XXII

THE OLD CODGER'S LAMENT

Who can say now,
"When I was young, the country was very beautiful?
Oaks and willows grew along the rivers
and there were many herbs and flowering bushes.
The forests were so dense the deer slipped through
the cottonwoods and maples unseen."

Who would listen?
Who will carry even the vicarious tone of that time?

In the old days
                age was honored.
Today it's whim,
                the whelp without habitat.

Who will now admit
                that he is either old or young
or knows anything?
All that went out with the forests.

XXIII

Trust me,
                    said the steady eyes
of the old wagon boss.
I'll get you to high ground
                                    and good water.

And he did!

That was the end
                    of an era.

XXIV

In this country
                     the sign outlives the prairie gopher.
Take it from me.
All you have to do is look at Goldfield, Nevada.
When the gold ran out,
                           everybody just walked off,
the gamblers and the whores first,
                             the owners next,
then the miners and the preacher.
                             But the sign still stands:
The Greatest Mining Camp the World Has Ever Known.

Yes sir, Goldfield, Nevada,
                       Population: one
abandoned company office,
                         one desk,
three paper clips,
                     two wire trays marked Incoming and Outgoing,
and one desk calendar
                     face-up on the guilty date,
all in the middle of nowhere . . . .
                       The Survivors!
You can't tell me that's not a sign.

You remember the insignia of Satchmo:
                          "Man, it's all in fun"?
Well, this was as straight-faced as a mule-head
                       on a pole.
You come on this thing at night
                     when you're not expecting it,
and I guarantee you won't touch another drop.

All this has been photographed now
                     for a historical society,
including one wall still standing of
                   The American Pool Room.
The windows are boarded up,
                 the door leans,
but the sign outside is still in perfect shape:
                   Coca Cola.

So there's no telling,
the signs may outlive America.

XXV

PHRASES THAT HAVE CHANGED AMERICAN HISTORY

Hoover . . .
      he was once President . . .
the compleat administrator . . .
            faceless and discreet
as a balloon . . .
      who never cracked a smile,
would you believe he once said,
      "There are only two occasions
when Americans respect privacy:
      prayer and fishing."

XXVI

LOVE AMERICA
UNCLE SAM NEEDS YOU

(Recruitment Poster)

I can love a dog,
                but a whole country
with interests bigger than death?
                              You gotta be kidding!
When you use *love* that way, uncle,
                      you mean to use me.

XXVII

THE COUNTRY SINGER

There ain't nothin special about me.
Everybody knows I'm too fat
and my legs are too short.
I'm just a middle-aged cornball
with a loud voice
and a drinking problem.
It's a funny thing,
when I'm on stage
all I do is act like me.
But I can act me
like a son of a bitch!

XXVIII

VERY SHORT POEM ON A RACING FORM

Wouldn't you know it?
                        Autobiography
won
      by a nose.

A lot
      of horse there!

XXIX

title for a historical painting

YOUNG BLACKS DEMONSTRATING IN FRONT OF
THE COUNTY COURTHOUSE

IN THE SILENT PORTICO THE ELDERS WATCH

XXX

THE VOICE OF THE PEOPLE

"Hell, what people?
                    Scruffy longhairs, that's who,
lying on their ass all day
                    or screwing,
expecting the government to take care of them.

Who's going to pay for all that,
                              Mr. Bleeding Heart?
Who's going to pay
                for all that?"

XXXI

THE WEIGHT LIFTER

When a man's
                    sweat
is strong
            enough to repel
mosquitoes,
                    boy,
that's character.

XXXII

FAMILY PORTRAIT, THREE GENERATIONS

all looking
            into the lens,
eyes wide,
            straight ahead:
holding!

"We're plain,
            we're church goers.

Who dares
            say anything
against that?"

XXXIII

NO PASARAN

Loyalist Rallying-Cry
Spanish Civil War

There's a guy
                at my shop
always telling me
                this ain't right
and that ain't right.
                It don't bother me none
he's a Red
                but what's the use of belly
achin all the time?

XXIV

NEW ORLEANS TRANSIENT BUREAU, 1934

Assigned
         a desk and an office
and their name on the door
                   for all to see:
James Watts, Social Worker,
                  secure,
and sitting before them
               a dependent, aimless human being,
impulses hitherto encysted
                 and out of sight
like the beautiful great seed
               of the avocado
gushed up
        warm
overflowing
          out to their shoulder blades,
great vibrations
          and depths,
compassion, sweet, bewildering,
                 resonant, man to man,
they were possessed by them
              as if they had heard a great muse
greater than reality itself,
           of trustworthy speech,
the muse of integrity
           calling to the applicant to respond,
and knew from their innermost being
that he and he and he,
          a man like everyone else
basically responsible,
        had to be helped!

To which
        (from a letter):
"All hope abandon ye
          who enter here
your hospitable annex
         on Bienville Street.

In the doorway the director.
'I'm George Selby,'
                    says he,
'I'm an official here.'

And I'm a seaman,
                    you crumb,
five notches above
                    any of you drifters.
I sailed up the Mississippi
when New Orleans was proud
                    of its merchant marine.

Yes, but you had your chance.
                    You failed.

Think what you like, Mr. Henk.
I must bear it.

Item:
        one tall man
club-footed,
                    with blue eyes
and no assets.

No assets?
            How do we know that?

By *looking* into these blue eyes, Mr. Henk.

Henk's eyes:
                If we help him
he might blow it
                    on booze.
He's a seaman.

A low blow, Mr. Henk.
                    Do what you want.
I can't stop you.

Rogan's eyes now to the fore:
                    He won't bare his soul.
How can we know

                    what we're dealing with?

Ouch!

R's eyes:
            or how to help him?

What can you do, Miss Rogan?

So it ended.
I was sent to Algiers
                    with the other saps
to be rehabilitated by work.
I remained what I am.
                    Like Henk.
Laughing and joking through it all.

Henk is awright.
                Hick!
Selby is awright.
                Hick!
You too, Miss Rogan.
You're awright."

ADDENDUM

In 1934 several hundred transients a day were pouring into the city of New Orleans, as into every large city in the country, ostensibly to look for work. They came leaping out of box cars and railroad gondolas and headed straight for the Transient Bureau where they knew they could get shelter, food and a shower.

Workers had long since given up looking for work, since there were no jobs anywhere and everybody knew it. These people were drifters and spongers looking for adventure. For the first time in the history of the country they had their own welfare agency and could speak up. Occasionally a bona fide worker would appear among them, battered, grim, ashamed, holding out on a spunk as irreducible as his bone structure. There were also those fleeing from anxiety and frustration, basically responsible men. But the others knew from their grapevine long before they reached New Orleans what questions would be asked of them, what they could expect, and how far they could go, and the game was to match wits and give those in charge a hard time.

The government had thrown this program together overnight in a desperate effort to curb transiency and help those who could be helped back on their feet. This would have been beyond any staff to achieve . . . this staff in particular.

There were very few trained social workers in the country at that time. In New Orleans there was only one in the whole agency. The others had to be recruited from the transients themselves and trained on the job. Anyone with two years of college and a responsible look was hired on the spot, without looking into work references, naturally, since these were people who had not been able to find jobs either. A more motley crew of hoi polloi was never seen in an agency staff. But they had one thing in their favor. They were too uninformed to realize how impossible their task was. All they had to work with was the interviewing process, which they had never done before, some petty cash, a shelter where the incoming transients were deloused, and Algiers, a large work camp where men could stay as long as a month or two if it was thought they needed to develop habits of work.

Selah!

DAY BOOK

If one could write like St. Augustine, not for the eyes of readers but for God, he would always give an honest accounting from the depths of his nature. But today one has to settle for the audience in one's self. It has the same standards, but it is mortal and easily intimidated. At the prospect of an outer audience, it immediately starts to play games. In that habitat one does not hear the supreme command to which the only response is from utter depth and fullness.

Today another intuitive grouping of words came to me. Something or other, I had written, "would agitate the Byzantine."

What Byzantine? Who was this somber figure and why mustn't I agitate him? Did the significance lie in the music of the words? A portentous secret lay locked in that phrase.

I had tried to work the Byzantine into a poem but his dignity loomed far above anything I could add. Next to him, the additions looked pale and small, and as if they didn't know what they were doing there. Apparently he was self-sufficient. But without additions, the phrase was not a poem. I could not, therefore, use the Byzantine. But I didn't have the heart to discard him, so I laid him out in prose for the intellect to dispose of.

In 1969 my attention was caught by a news story describing the great scientific machinery that had to be installed in the National Archives to protect the Declaration of Independence and the Constitution against mouldering. I recognized at once the presence of a poem, but for some reason which I can't remember now, all I did was jot down the facts and throw them into a folder of notes. When I came across them a year later, I was ready to make the poem. By some inexorable, almost automatic process, the longer I worked at it, the more different it became from the facts, until all resemblance had disappeared. Then I was satisfied. I had written "Americana XXI."

Braque had already had this experience when he noted, A painting is finished when the idea in it has been obliterated.

This is the poem. It was written in a few minutes. Even that seemed too long, for I remember feeling bored . . . yes, bored . . . and annoyed at being tied up on something that meant so little to me. Yet it has irreducible and exact tone no matter how many times I read it, which is more than I can say for my poems of feeling, which long to be as unchanging and tone-absolute as a machine.

"XXI   AMERICANA

lies in a glass
                    and bronze
case

indecipherable
                    sealed

in helium
                    under the eyes
of a black
                    guard
in the National Archives

and is lifted ineluctably
                                        on electric jacks
from an underground tale."

"How quickly the dandelions
come up
            after a rain.
I picked them
            all
only yesterday."
            (from "A Reminder of William Carlos Williams")

These dandelions came from my front lawn. I stood in disbelief, staring at them dully and saying to myself the ordinary homeowner words of the poem. The next thing I remember was becoming aware that their meaning was complete and that there was something fundamental and permanent about the situation. This gave the words, of no

94

interest in themselves, an enhanced significance which began to excite me. It began to feel like a poem. I hung on.

The next thing I remember was the realization that this was exactly the kind of thing Williams would have noticed and reported. This made the experience possibly interesting enough for a poem, and I already had the only title it could honestly have, "A Reminder of William Carlos Williams." All this took less than a minute. What remained was to work out the line arrangement on the typewriter. When I had done that, however, I was still dissatisfied. There was not enough there.

I hung on. Time dragged. It began to look as if there was no way to connect with what was missing. But my subconscious, which had been guiding me, would not let go and traced the final connection: it was that this way of looking at things had become an American mode. And so I called it an "Americana." Now the poem looked as if it had range and a solid base.

The special characteristic of the very short poem is that the reader has to be hit before he realizes he's been shot. But for this to happen, the author, in the writing of it, also has to be hit before he realizes he's been shot.

I had precisely this experience in writing "Old Hickory." I had come across this order that Stonewall Jackson had given his men at the Battle of New Orleans and was immediately struck by the words, "Elevate them guns a little lower!" and jotted them down for possible use later. That time came when I was working on something else and happened to glance across at the scrap of paper on which the words were written. The poem just wrote itself then from the words. In it I was simply acknowledging that I had been shot. But I had already been hit when I read the quotation. Fortunately I reacted before my intellect and my counterwill had a chance to realize that there was a job to be done.

Not unlike perhaps what happens to a sculptor when something in a piece of stone attracts him and he chips away at it until he sees what it is. At that point the concept . . . the "poem" in the stone . . . is completed. The rest is technique.

"One thing about a persona, it has no spermatozoon, but the spermatozoon does have the gene for a persona."

Writing this, I felt I had made a profound discovery. On a second look, however, the meaning had disappeared. *Of course* a persona had no spermatozoon. What I had had in mind was the state in which a persona behaves like a real person in a poem and that how it gets into such a state is a mystery, since no one witnesses its passage. Yet there it is, acting as if it had forgotten that it was only a persona and would now rise to the greatest heights. This is when the poem is in greatest danger, I had meant to warn, for it is this inflated sense which calls on grandiosity and on those two horsemen of abdication, rhetoric and abstraction, and which creates the illusion that nothing is beyond it and that it needs nothing more from the real world.

But why sound such an alarm when the indistinctness between *persona* and *persona into real* is precisely the mystery on which poetry feeds?

All this started with two words, *persona* and *eye*, which I had scribbled along with others on a scrap of paper, preparatory to a poem. The poem was written, but a day or two later, I was looking for something on my desk and noticed the two words, this time as possibly connected in a deep sense. How I got from *eye* to *spermatozoon*, I don't know. Perhaps I paired them subconsciously because they are both real in a physical sense in contrast to *persona*. At the end, it turned out that I never left the word, *eye*, for what I wrote here was the work of the intellect, also an eye.

The feelings (to the poet): Why have you abandoned me?

        one goes blank into an obsessive, cold universe
        one makes associations to solid objects
        one turns into abstraction, which like the orchid seems to feed on air

I have never been able to remember, even in analysis, what I felt as a boy of six when I parted from my grandmother in Hungary. I never knew my mother, nor knew why not; nor my father either, since he had left to settle in the States when I was only a year old. My grandmother, therefore, was my mother, but more gentle and kind than a mother.

Her presence has always been with me. There is only one like her. The eyes are sad and reflective, the face tired, beginning to show wrinkles, but the mouth smiles and an incomparable sweetness, her character, exudes from her, holding nothing back, and envelops me. She leans towards me, attentive, smiling, and I respond in like, as I had learned to do from her, also smiling, all inside me light.

Now my father had remarried and this woman had come to take my brother and me back with her to America, where I had never been. I do not know now whether I suspected that I would never see my grandmother again but I did know it was an important parting, yet all I remember of that last day is the hustle and bustle and a great silence and my extraordinary calm and robustness of spirit.

I found the explanation for this many years later in a passage of a book. The author was describing how the political prisoners in a Siberian detention camp during the Stalin terror managed to preserve their sanity. "The main thing," she wrote, "was in a certain self-control: it was important not to think about the future. Expect nothing and be ready for anything. The only other thing was to scream, but no one would have heard." (Nadezhda Mandelstam, *Hope Against Hope*)

With that formula I managed my transition to America quite well. But my poor grandmother, what was there for her to hold on to?

I can imagine the final moment. The bags are packed. We are all dressed, ready to leave. The time has come. All I am thinking of is the going and the necessity to act as if this were like any other day. I walk up to her and like my granddaughter, Julie, also six, let myself be hugged and kissed with that self-possession and vigilance which protect children. And I leave without recognizing her grief or even acknowledging that this is a separation.

Forgive me.

THE MANDOLIN LESSON, A DREAM

"Have you done what I told you?"
                          asked my father,
long after I had stopped writing poetry.
He had recommended a methods book
                          on the mandolin.

"No, but I remember
                its name, *La Méthode!*"
My French articulation
                    was exact and fluent.
I was in good spirits.

Somewhere in the background,
                          not visible,
he heard
          and perked up.
His voice was stronger
                    than in the past.
"Listen to the Hungarian!"
                    he cried to my mother, delighted,
then said it in French
                    but it was unbelievably long
and heavy
          like interlocked German gutturals.
We all laughed.
                Incredible!

He was very old now,
                I reflected,
and had spoken
                in an absolute, level voice,
not his,
          thinking only of my welfare.
He knew that I would need
                          something creative.

So, a foreboding:
                after he was gone,
I would remember

　　　　　　　　　　　he had really cared
and would grieve.

I awoke then.

　　Obviously I was being told why I had stopped
writing. The mandolin was the symbol.
　　I did have a mandolin when I was a boy. We were
very poor then and I had to save pennies from my weekly
allowance to get one. But lessons were far beyond our means,
so I taught myself to play from instruction books, which was
not unusual in those days. My father neither approved nor
disapproved, but when he heard that I wanted to be a poet,
he was troubled. He didn't see how I could earn a living, and
since I didn't know either, we could never talk about it. He
was a gentleman, though, and didn't try to stop me. What I
did, therefore, I had to do without his encouragement.
　　The dream changed all that. This time around, he
did encourage me. "Listen to the Hungarian!" he had cried
with delight when he heard my fluent French, meaning by
that, as a Hungarian, "Look at that crazy Hungarian go!"
This time, however, it was I who didn't follow through and
apply myself. The reason was in my father's German, which
in the dream was incredibly long and heavy and interlocked
. . . the way I actually felt about writing. My speaking
French was another way of explaining why I had stopped
writing: "It was all like a foreign tongue to me." In this
language of incomprehension I was fluent, the dream said.
But it also tried to keep up my spirits by reassuring me that I
had not lost *all* touch with writing, I could still remember the
name of the book that could lead me to it and at least
pronounce the words of this foreign language.
　　The dream then moved to my father's later years
when he and I had become quite close. He was now the good
father who had had his son's welfare at heart all along and
had always wanted him to be a poet, knowing that this was
what he needed. As proof of this, he had spoken in "an
absolute, level voice, not his." This did not mean that this time
he had said what he really meant, for a more honest man
never lived. It was simply a way of emphasizing the point . . .
like saying, "on the level" . . . at the same time acknow-
ledging that this was not really the way things had been.
　　The meaning was now unmistakable. Look, the

99

dream said, if you're going to attribute your writing problem to a lack of early encouragement, we'll replay this whole thing. We'll make your father encouraging and interested this time and you'll see, it wouldn't have made any difference. You still wouldn't have applied yourself.

Of course, I had already realized this. I had seen through my stratagem and been amused at it. That's why the dream at first was so playful and gay. It just wanted to make sure that I knew and to dispel any lingering doubt.

There was something in the dream, though, that I could not take so lightly. It was the inertness of my will. It all came from my father. Thus, I was able to by-pass my agony.

How dependent I am on analogy for understanding! Like the scientist.

When the going is rough, I find myself speaking first and then trying to figure out what it means. This suggests that the natural character of language is intuitive and is *made* communicative and functional afterwards.

I have the uneasy feeling that we have been conned by ingenious stylists.

A voice comes for a poem, released by writing from subconscious depths. The speaker is never seen but his heraldic device is. Nothing is known about him but that.

If I look at anything long and hard, I wind up seeing only its inaccessibility, the mystery of its nature.

But is the mystery really out there or in my own nature?

100

Chance and indeterminacy are not where I hurt or where my impotence matters. But surrealism would have us believe that that *is* where we live . . . in fortuitous images, exciting and singular. The trouble is, all those millions of images add up to nothing.

On reading the early philosophers on the nature of being, I exclaimed, "How rich and wonderful is the character of speculation! pure poetry."

I am not altogether honest when I write. I find myself giving up my intentions for beauty of phrase.

I would like to write a play but I have no wish to move people around. My heart goes out to them the way they are. I want only to experience and cohabit them.
And I have no interest in entertaining anybody.

If it's not clearer than prose, I tell myself, it's prose no matter how it's arranged on the page, but I'm afraid I'm just repeating an elitist echo.

How intractable the subject! But that only gives it depth and mystery, which are all I need to feel lyrical.

Inhibition, that is the problem. Always. Once I've broken through, I'm back where I started and another poem is needed to break through again.

I too long for Utopia but without believing that it could include the poets.

When George Oppen first read my poem, "In Thy Sleep / Little Sorrows Sit And Weep," it seemed to him that if it had ended on the line, "the crow slept," it would have been "absolutely immovable." By that he meant so solid that it couldn't be reduced any further.

The strange thing is that ending the poem there ends it before anything has happened. *That* poem looks into eternity in a very different way. It is as if nature, and the poem, were more self-contained and clairvoyant when they were still, and had more gravitational pull and magic while they were still brooding and imminent.

I keep telling myself that it makes no sense whatever to feel that prose is inferior to poetry, but it's no use.

I've never had a really good idea that didn't start with feeling. And a really good image has never come to me except by accident. My destiny lies in the hands of these two.

When I look up from my chair at the books in my study, I feel the way Atlas must have felt when he touched earth. Before I settle down to work, I touch them with my eyes (I still remember the excitement I felt as a boy when I first walked into a public library) and feel tiny, inner exclamations inexpressibly sweet, like the impulse to a prayer or the frisky little kick of a lamb. I know then that it's all right to go ahead.

Why should I not acknowledge this? I am not ashamed to be sentimental. My books glow. I have been with them longer than with my children and grandchildren, in a magic wood where I have found identity. Together we are sufficient.

Yet many of them I have not read. Was it because I

like to leave the best to the last? or because the moment never seemed right? Now I shall never read them. There isn't time if I'm going to find out what there is in me.

My imagination gives me the illusion of being able to transcend myself further and further.

O radiant magnetic lode, are you trying to tell me something by this?

You have the strangeness of the preconscious.

You yearn to make a soul, while the soul, formless, yearns to have a body.

Only honesty and compassion, o imagination, can make you habitable.

I can not move in on a mystery in a straight line. I have to pretend that I am motionless and not looking, and invent a voice, nominally outside, which it will feel safe to approach and play out its nature in a suppositional world.

This is the same place where all the bastards of the world are brought before the bar of justice and get their final come-uppance.

A passage from Maritain follows me around: to him poetry meant "that intercommunication between the inner being of things and the inner being of the human self which is a form of divination."

"Look out for another windmill, my dreamy master," warns Sancho Panza. "Things are not that easily divined. They remain self-contained and imperturbable. You can't hear a peep out of them no matter what you divine. They don't agree or disagree with anything."

Nevertheless, my heart agrees with Maritain, for it loves matter more than poetry itself and longs for some divination of it, to be close to its inner being, and where the heart longs, the imagination has already been, Sancho or no Sancho, to get its bearings first, feeling with metaphors, trying

103

out figures of speech in the blank.

Was there already a response in them?

In any case, the poet has a special license for this mystical, uncharted mission, which the ancients regarded so highly that the Oracles of Delphos themselves were delivered in verse.

Along now come the physicists and lay it all out, cold, the structure of matter. Just the physical model and the topography of forces. And *that* is as rich as metaphor; yet still no closer to the inner being than a dismembered body on a dissecting table is to feeling.

So quiet, Sancho!

I had an assignation with the spirit of man but I was weak and in love with the spirit of language and kept him waiting.

EX CRANIUM,
THE POET

Why should the experience in a poem be secondary to the writing? It looks wrong.

But if it were not, how could the act of writing be a full experience?

Aye, there's the rub!

What elevated feelings a metaphor can produce! what mysterious excitement, despite its depersonalization! Nevertheless it's best to proceed cautiously with it the way Ulysses dealt with Circe, by first fortifying himself with a root. Only then did he live with her and beget children before returning to Penelope.

The more impossible the problem, the more poetical the possibilities. An ideal situation.

The poetic impulse is romantic because it is aspirational and idealistic. The mind, always venturesome, craves new modes, but the alternatives turn out to be essays or mere games and diversions.

There are poems in which the experience feels as if it had barely managed to pass through a poor conductor and had come out wood. Any resemblance to a poem is due entirely to language and imagination.

This does not mean, however, that they should be judged purely as invention. That would be unsuited to the haunting depth and mystery of poetry's character, which are not attained by language and imagination alone. The dark vibrancy which sends shivers down the spine is grounded in a referent from the real world.

A voice comes to the poet, feeling its way, speaking

107

to no one, but on the page it enters into a relationship with the reader as if it were a person.

The mind and the imagination are so rapid that they seem to start with a conclusion and leave no trace of how they got there. It is not surprising, therefore, that we have attributed this feat to a higher power, like the Muse, and that our conventional symbol is a bird.

The mind's instant facility for going past human feelings into the purely architectonic works on poetry the way geologic time works on a bird: the poem comes out bone-clean on the page, looking like the faint outline of an imperishable pterodactyl.

The voice Blake heard had such physical presence that it crossed over into another sense, purring like a tiger, and gave the illusion that it had not passed through the intellect. How great were both the presence and the illusion!

Poetry hankers to be something that has never been seen before, to make fine shadings and ideal forms beyond understanding, and to sing and epitomize and be beautiful for all time.

For all this, naturally, it expects to be admired.

Prose is more flesh and blood. You don't have to reduce it to essentials. It goes at a walking pace, the way a man breathes and meditates. In addition, anything can go into it. It is plain and open to everybody. That feels good.

The imagination, not being a function of character, which does not vary greatly among men, is not bound by its specificity. Hence, it is practically inexhaustible.

Thus, even a mediocre poet can be original, but the further he goes down the road of pure imagination, the further he will be from existential questions. Which may be why the pure products of the imagination have a hard quiddity, and innovation in time becomes boring and depressing, like an assembly line endlessly spitting out new gadgets.

Poetry, like metaphysics, craves to find something permanent behind changing appearances, some yet unknown form of a transcendent nature.

When Kant held that there were fixed postulates which *had* to be, he was assigning a habitat and a character to their form in the mind itself, since the assertion could only have been made as a response to some inner form, some modality, in his own mind.

We have only a dim sense, as in side vision, of the presence of these forms, shadowy colossi through which we pass. In the world of absolutes they become seemingly as clear as matter. If, for example, I say, Evil must exist because Good exists and there always has to be an opposite to Good, what I am saying is that this idea exists as a pair of eternal antipodes: if you have one, you must have the other because one has meaning only in relation to the other. The mind is incapable of thinking in any other modality.

Yet ideas also exist on their own. Two and two make four, no matter what, not only because it is the mind's modality but because nature itself conforms and lets itself be manipulated by it.

The indefatigable dreaming of absolutes is in the mainstream of human nature, therefore, and their form in poetry corresponds to what is already dimly a form in the poet's mind and nature. The poetic impulse is the yearning to get to this inner modality.

No wonder a poem on a page looks independent and absolute. It is.

Prose: you can take your shoes off in it, fellah, and

109

light a pipe.
>It hops from thing to thing like a pecking
>sparrow.
>It stays within limits and knows what's
>good for it (must be congenial to nature).

Poetry just looks good. That's enough.

Strange that the English language, which is so big on poetry, has no appropriate words to express its nature. Thus, poems are said to be "lyrical," as if they gave off the sound of a lyre or a song; or to have an "inner music," in recognition of its inward character. And poems are called cantos, fugues, songs, symphonies. It is as if we were stopped at the borders of the physical, from where music emanates, and had to describe what takes place on the other side by what is known on the physical side.

It is a sloppy business, for poetry's "inner music" bears no resemblance to the sound of an instrument, and if you try to sing it, you know at once that you are in the wrong medium. The truth is, a poem starts in the reader's memory. There the words are assigned sound, pace, stress, rhythm, phrasing, intonation, etc., from the spoken language. This part is physical and can be compared to music. While this is going on, however, one is also making literary and personal associations with the words, reflecting on their sense, responding to their emotion . . . all of which lie outside music . . . so that when you read a poem like Blake's "Evening Star," the ear is immediately full of a bursting ecstasy of "inner music." But the burst is the instantaneous *combination* in the mind, and the ecstasy is the reaction to the quality of its balance, measure, integralness, and to a robustness in the elements. In their presence the reader has become an instrument. This makes him feel so good, he could sing. But to speak of this as music is a bit of poetizing.

He who reveals the consequences of society on himself leaps across the intervening distance.

110

Regarding fragmentation in contemporary poetry, some poets seem incapable, for physiological reasons perhaps, to make a synapse; and some are riding an avant garde wave, letting the whole mind hang out, which in its free state, with its inexhaustible novelties, is fragmentary.

Those who claim, however, that poets are that way because the world is that way, mistake their hysteroid impulses for reality. The natural response to a state of uncertainty is tighter, more vigilant integration, not less. Otherwise we could not cope with danger.

There is no end to the pseudo-experience which our auxiliaries in culture are willing to forgive in the name of art. And why should there be an end as long as they equate dissociation with originality and believe that poetry is a self-contained intellectual game whose object is superiority?

The fact is that it takes as much honesty to write a durable poem as imagination and craftsmanship. The longing for *altogether* honest, *personal* expression is so strong that if a poem has it, we are willing to forgive its shortcomings.

There are little poems about ordinary things which are as strong as an epic without raising their voice, but they have this power not because they are modest or about ordinary things but because a discriminating mind, the kind that is adept at metaphysical first causes, has sifted out the essence of a thing, and that is epic.

It is a long time since it could be said of an American poet that he touched the heart. The odd and terrifying thing is that this is not noticed.

Must we settle for poetry as the cold art or but a figuration of the mind? Why should it be less than man himself?

Scale in the *Cantos* is in inverse proportion to expressive power.

If you could get down to its essence, even a turnip would be poetic.

What is remarkable is that poetry can prove it.

As soon as the poem as it is to be begins, the character of language looms in the way. That is when the poem is first experienced as an object.

CASE HISTORIES

X's experiences are sincerely felt but not objectified. The result is awful because it is not the experience in a poem which provides the main interest . . . experiences are not *that* different from each other . . . but the nature of the objectification.

Y's experiences, on the other hand, are thoroughly and ingeniously objectified but the experience conveyed in the "object" moves very feebly. The impression is that the experience, sincere as far as it went, was not thoroughly felt and that the whole person was not involved. Therefore not all of the reader is involved. He has to settle for Y's intelligence and skill, which are sufficient to be interesting and pleasurable. But when it is all over, what he *feels* is a dud, despite the brilliant display.

MODES AGAINST AN IRRESISTIBLE ADVERSARY

The Passive: the sweetness of fragility; the tear just short of a whimper; the song. Yeats.

The Olympian: Pound: *he* deals the cards, contained and imperturbable.

The Dramatic: Eliot: locates the suffering in time and place and composes its drama.

Language as an Alternative: Stevens.

ANTIBODIES

The poet *getting into shape*	First, the blood vessels in the area of a wound expand.
His imagination rushes *to an idea*	Blood and plasma rush in like rescue squads with highly mobile white cells from the bone marrow.
The throes of writing	The microbes multiply; the leucocytes swarm to the defense.
The medium	Some surround the infection and make a wall with their own bodies.
He makes his thrust	The rest fall upon the enemy
and exhausts his subject	and eat them.
Images lose their lives *in the process*	But some die.
Finally, the poem!	Their bodies, together with the microbes and the damaged tissue form a white pus (very apt for Sylvia Plath).
And the moral.	If the battle extends too far, the lymph nodes become overloaded and swollen.

In poetry originality is needed in somewhat the same way that a man needs a personality. He can have everything else and still look academic as hell without it. For this reason, and because originality also has something to do with being able to let out *all* the organ stops, the poet with a passive, compliant character never quite makes it, however skillful and knowing his craftsmanship.

If after a writer's death only historians remain interested in his originality, that only means it has entered the mainstream and become so familiar, it is no longer noticed.

The preoccupation with it, therefore, is not just a modern neurosis.

The practice of ranking poets as major and minor, the bastard offspring of grading students, freezes the poet in his tracks and makes him a nobody if he is less than great. This situation tempts him unduly into lofty postures, the breeding ground of rhetoric and abstraction, and intimidates his most precious asset, his individuality.

What does ranking have to do with poetry anyhow? The term, *major*, when it is not a sales gimmick, is the creation of those who like the power of dispensing judgment or need a medium in which to display their intellectual talent.

It has become a great plaything and a way to silence poetry and put it away.

This world has more parrots than the jungles of Brazil.

The trouble with social subjects is that there is only one response to them and that has already been made. It is not the poet in us who is stirred by them but the humanitarian. The poet is stirred only when he can make his own alternatives and has free play for idiosyncrasy and invention.

All that a neurosis can do for a poem is to reproduce itself in such a way as to be either exorcised or reassured.

The New Hedonism: If a writer feels empty and down in the dumps, he announces to the world that the proper subject matter of poetry is disaster.

Poetry works on the same basic assumption as sympathetic magic, that an image and a ceremony will bring about an effect beyond ordinary means. Thus, it is not hyperbole to speak of a poem's magic.

Ever since Rimbaud we have been acting as if the reader were a monkey on our backs, trying to shake him off. Perhaps we had no alternative but to declare our emancipation from his psychology and theorize that a poem must be judged by different criteria once we realized we were alone in our aleatory imagination and had lost all hope that the ordinary reader could walk that road. No matter, the fact remains that once a poem is written, it can *be* anything only in the mind of a reader. His psychology, therefore, can never be dismissed.

This fact prevents us from ranging too far from our own nature.

Ideas for poems . . . these bastards live for adulation or to radiate into the mind. If you so much as look the other way for a second, they're gone.

Between those poets who shoot from the hip of intuition and those who labor in the intellect, there can be no detente. It is not simply a matter of taste or judgment; it is a personality difference so basic that it feels as if survival depends on killing off the other side. This is done with scorn or by dispensing judgments as if the other side did not exist.

It is sometimes necessary to talk about craftsmanship in order to show that poetry is not outside the pale, that it too is rational and responsible and has a handle to its nature.

A word to the tragedian poet: don't try to convince me. Just be sad.

Nobody seems to believe any more that the true poet is the lyrical poet and has to fight against his own intellect. Nobody gives a damn about that.

There is no actual body in a Dylan Thomas poem over which the tone weeps. Hence, the strong, hypnotic cadence gives it a sickly hue.

Surrealism can be forgiven for being so gloomy and uninhabitable; even for preferring zombies to reality. But not for excluding the mystical too. When you leave both out, there is nothing left but the chicken-scribblings of a Martian.

There is a great hunger for modesty. Apparently we feel comfortable with a poet only when he is comfortable with his limitations.

Noble, universal subjects have to draw on rhetoric because they do not issue from direct experience and do not, therefore, have its language at their disposal.

The feeling of exaltation which the thought of

utterance induces, as if there were a bird in utterance itself
. . . not much can be done with just that. Hence, poems are
about other things, but it is kept as the concealed subject. One
does not, after all, want to scare the bird off. Besides, there
are moments when that is all we care for.

Men escape from realistic limitations on the wings of
an artist's fortunate intuitions about his medium.

Yet what does *form* mean? I do not even know what
it means to ask the question. All I know is that when I ask it, I
am in the existential world and that it can only be answered
there. The answer may, in fact, *be* the existential world.

In time romantic poetry becomes sickening. What
was once a great surge of longing becomes too much of a good
thing; becomes in time merely lingual and automatic. A
clean-up crew then comes in and strips it down. The object
thereby comes into view. The puritans are congratulated on
their discovery. People again feel exhilarated and hopeful. But
the plain, honest product palls in time and does not satisfy the
heart. So a new generation of rebels rediscovers the romantic,
but it is not called that because it has a different set of
manners and cues. Anyhow, it too in time loses credibility.
And so it goes.

Specificity pulls the most profound-looking ideas
down to earth.

The short lyric is not admired these days despite the
fact that it liberates the reader from his substantive ex-
pectations.

Individuality remains avant garde.

117

One of the poets has discovered how to write as if he were already embalmed. The vocabulary, meticulous, looks as simple as table and chairs, but its dry, a-rational combinations suggest another dimension. It is so distilled of everything felt on earth, including noumenon, that it sends chills down the back. That is its hubris, and greatly impresses critics.

What a man won't do to free himself from the influence of other poets!

There is a poetry for the individual architecture of each poet's mind.

The poet is more modest than the ancient philosopher: he doesn't claim that what he has thought out is the ultimate reality. On the other hand, what philosopher would be so foolish and pretentious as to claim that philosophy is what some poets claim poetry is, prophecy?

Not enough distinction is made between metaphors which transform a subject into poetry and those in which a poet escapes from his subject.

It is flattering to have a composer write music for one's poems, but they already have a music of their own!

There is an early poem by Tristan Tzara in Rumanian, "Song of War," as plain and straightforward as a peasant. The words are so honest that even in translation they sound as if a whole people were speaking, and one forgets that they were written by a man.

All that Dada trickery afterwards. What a waste!

Each poem should be an independent little island, independent, that is, to the eye, but not of the reader. Why should I assume that he loves little islands less than I?

A poem is exciting when it has a very still center; perhaps because language in its everyday state is fluid.

If a poet is gifted, there are some distinct advantages to being slightly paranoid. In fact, one can make a great name for oneself in that way. This is because we are Americans and endow energy with charisma, in the arts particularly from the compression boiler of a paranoia still within workable bounds, whose figurations it has become a vogue to regard as the character of the modern condition. And not without reason, for our nerves have been badgered so long by news reports that a sense of something ominous, perhaps cataclysmic has crossed the threshold and inclines us in that direction. In this vogue the only question is whether the figurations are well done.

Furthermore, there are things in this state which do actually work in the interests of art. The principal one is the paranoidal bind itself which locks a person into this system and forces him to work as a faithful servant to its exigencies. Since he can't get out, he can't be diverted by anything outside. Consequently all he has to do is follow the messages he is receiving in order to have perfect psychological consistency, dead certainty, inevitability, in the sense that he *has* to do this, and deadly accuracy, a combination of such great power that it produces artistic shivers which others can achieve only by the greatest insight and discipline.

In addition, from the inside boiler comes an intensity that passes for passion, and a brilliance as if the poet himself was in the flames of his agony and struggle.

This inner world, as everyone knows, is apocalyptic —and that is enough to make any man's fortune, for who doesn't know that this world is visionary and profound and that its lone figure is a magus?

Needless to say, all this is too much to resist. The reader succumbs into *folie à deux.* One is safe only if he has perceived that this is a closed system and that the magus is a prisoner unable to let anything in from the outside that doesn't satisfy his master—no dialectic, no self-understanding, no compassion, no humor—and that the system is not related to what is going on outside: it assumes *it* is what is going on there. Thus, the only thing it tells about the human condition is its own skewed condition.

What nobody seems to want to talk about is that there *is* a distinction, the significance of which is obvious once it is made, between the way in which the imagination and the mind work when they are under orders from an obsession and the way they work in an open field, as in *Finnegans Wake*, where anything is possible to one who has the means.

To be sure, there is fascination in being locked in with all that power, with a magus, but if one doesn't have the constitution for entering a paranoidal system, one might still be able to get a kick out of it, as a form of tragedy—another case of man the victim of his obsession—or as entertainment if one has a taste for horror movies.

The arts are a monument to man's inventiveness in counteracting temporality, his above all, by ends in them-selves.

There is no greater organ than the eye but a poem can take only so much of it, after which, the more visual a poem the more desolate and unreal until one feels like vomiting and every bone in the body cries out, "Does a man not have an ear and a heart too?"

The finished poem: "Ah, free at last from psychology!"

THE ARTIST

This letter will be off and on. Am much into work, getting ready for my February show, but as usual am dragging. It's all a complex cross-weave here, with children, college, etc. . . . painting dominant. Wish you could stand with me in front of my new things and we could talk. So much has passed into them. I've been changed too.

The thing you like, the "given" quality of nature, the forces that are in the earth, how I'd love my work to have these! But I have to work through conception and contrivance, my force is there. If that works, it acquires a nature of its own, it seems to me, which then is as if it were a given, don't you think?

You were right about the obsessiveness of my lines. Apparently I tense up and hold my brush so tight when I paint / concentrate that my whole right side gets tied into knots. Am on some muscle relaxant now. This letter gives my eye and hand a chance to rest. I must get back to work, though, in a minute.

But going back to what you said, I too think that the genesis of art is a query / desire for "the nature of being." The surprising thing is that this should become the motive for inventing one's self and give such a lift to it.

I wrote a friend this morning, "In life the only ending is death. That is why I have to endure this raging of chaos and will in me until I can shape it into art."

God, how time goes! What a bad correspondent I am.

Have been in a poor way. Very active on the surface, a small hell underneath. The doctor put me on dexamil. Suddenly *it* lifted and I began to work. It all flew so fast, I couldn't finish. I must re-feel it all. It *has* to be real.

Dear Carlos, excuse my narcissism.

No painting. State of death.

In addition, an old affaire with a young man is breaking up. He's been a drain on me. Still, I need him, and I keep asking, "Why deny myself?" And an older man . . . very nice . . . known him for years . . . is separating from his wife

123

and turning to me. But he's not an artist. That frightens me. Would it be another spin-away from my work? Everything seems so fragile. Am terrified of the hold a man might get over my life.

My therapist is no help. Just looks on and says we quarrel. This only makes me more incoherent and propels me faster towards a crash of some kind. But am looking forward to the Christmas holidays. What a joy it will be . . . the connection to a canvas again, the quiet attention to feeling, the concentration.

Wish you were close by so we could talk.

Not able to write until now, too many things to do . . . shopping for jackets, calling the service station, mending pants, making tuna sandwiches, quartermastering boots / mufflers / long underwear, carrying small boys to bed, taking temperatures, etc., etc. On top of everything the rotating chairmanship of the Department! Tiresome, tiresome. Not *into* anything. See no one but colleagues.

Yet too many feelings. Loving by phone, not knowing where it will lead.

Funny, being a woman: one provokes actions but does not let them happen.

Worst of all, no painting. Semester an oblivion.

Write! Imperative. Hugs.

P.S. I don't recognize myself in my words, they're so dismal. Painting holds my sense best.

Be patient with me.

A reprieve. Boys off with their grandmother. Have been painting madly, day and night, for five days now. For a show coming up. Four more oils to finish. The fingers, the eyes, the neck, the spine are ready to strike, but the will . . . ha! . . . the will won't let them.

Actually, I don't have anything to write. It's all going into painting. I just snatched a moment from it . . . I was painting a white line on a field that was somewhere on the short south wall when we saw each other there last . . . in order to keep in touch. I can't bear winds of annoyance.

It's cold here. Color changes by the hour.

Nervous feelings: my work needs critical attention to make it last. How I long for that.

Think kindly of me. I'm smiling at you and see you smile back.

P.S. Wallace Stevens, the part of him that's eye, yes! I know what you mean about his being rhetorical but maybe he's that way because he's not looking for answers.

I'm still painting. Total obliteration. The work as insistent as the force of gravity. Its specificity: isn't that *it* altogether? Would we know life if there weren't the tooth, the bite, the burr? When I can't attend to that kind of detail, I know I'm sick.

It's hard to say who my favorite painters are. I look hard at all of them to see what they are about.

The mountains were purple yesterday. Snow on them now, raining below. Clouds bluish-grey, heavy, embroiled.

Much concern here about drugs. The tribal cry, "Something has to be done!" Eyes must see; not the disengaged stare of the addict . . . that's insane. The mind must care. We are not just spectators in a ritual theatre.

If I could see you and put my hand on your arm, things would be more tolerable.

A short holiday on the beach. I used to ride the hand-carved horses and Roman chariots on the merry-go-round here and watch the night lights off the pier. Long afterwards they reappeared in a painting I did in a N.Y. studio. At the time I thought it was a pure abstraction but there they were, the night lights, changed very little.

I used to pick crepe myrtle and flowering hawthorn near here. In the evening we used to drive through the cemetery where my grandmother is buried. How alive I felt walking through that marked place in internal talk.

In a few days the new semester starts and "it" all begins again!

How self-centered I am! It's terribly embarrassing.

125

When I was little, grandmother used to put a hood over her canary's cage to calm it. Who will do that for me? or release me from my mill tasks? Around and around I go like a donkey, further and further from childhood.

You told me to look into people's faces and listen to what they were saying to me . . . "to get what is really out there" . . . but, my God, they don't know themselves. They act like tropisms. Or am I too engrossed in my own body sensations . . . the smell of grass, stuffed sinuses, all the things I have to see as a painter . . . to attend to what is not me?

I've been stewing in loneliness. Everyone is out of reach. I had a friend once but she moved away. We used to weep together. But I can't do that with others. It would be too revealing, too deranged.

Last night I was working on a painting, yellow on black, and at 4 a.m. became very ill with chills and fever. I vomited. It was a searing, transparent yellow, impacting both red and green. Bile, grandmother used to call it.

Beautiful day. Everything a painting: the inexpressible light, the hues of sky and tree interacting. Then a good game of tennis. In the evening a concert . . . violin, piano, cello . . . so sweet, my eyes glazed. Boys with me, becoming men, a joy to see.

Paintings grow up too and go off on their own, after vagueness has been willed into them, as in a rock, a tree, a cloud.

Excuse this outpouring but I feel very safe with you. Maybe that means I've been feeding on your understanding and taken advantage of you. Now it's your turn. Write me everything. Don't be afraid.

A day at the lake: breezy, grey. Thunderheads appear, pink / orange; sounds waterfalling; the boys walking on the white shore. In the distance, pine and goldenrod and a green pasture. All in proportion. A divine parity.

Silver grey and blue on the water moving into image

and reflection. A fish jumps. The concentric circles spread.

In the late afternoon, more intense contrasts: greens and pinks deeper, the water quieter, still more grey. The hour has lost its full measure. Into the fall chill.

Here comes Peter running across the sand. I'm smiling. Oh, the long, perpetual highs of a seven year old!

If only one could always be simple. But I'm too sentimental for that.

Have been seeing a young writer friend and having long, endearing talks over the phone with old buddies (married men), but it's all very unsatisfactory. I seem to have a loose live-wire in me somewhere.

Yesterday I was invited out to dinner by a couple of young colleagues and wound up cooking dinner for them, they got so drunk, and feeling cross at myself for allowing it. I hate being used. I want people to be concerned about *me*.

I do seem to be awkward with men, don't I? I seem to set off things in them that make me damn nervous. Like that phone call this morning at 3 a.m. A young trembly voice:
"I love you."
"What?"
"Don't you recognize my voice?"
"No."

Is this live-wire thing dangerous to you?

OBSERVATIONS

"In the beginning the Word was
and the Word was with God
and the word was God."
This astonishing Platonism from the New Testament
corresponds to our intuitive sensations about utterance, and
our very soul is laid bare in "Heaven and earth shall pass away
but my words shall not."

If art were only a matter of the imagination, it
would always be surrealist and would soon be a drag, for the
imagination is aleatory and its pure products as hard and self-
contained as plastic.

A thing can be described, but what it is can not be
rendered except by variations of itself. Man, however, is not
satisfied with this. He is more obdurate than nature. Thus his
own character is the mother of metaphysics and poetry.

The real subject of the avant-garde theatre is a sense
of void and inchoateness in an unconcerned universe. This
void has no counterpart in nature, however, or in the human
consciousness. Indeed, when *consciousness* feels low its
impulse is the opposite. It rushes in like nature to fill the
threatening vacuum; it fills the whole world, in fact. No, this
theatre has made a clean break with nature. This gives it its
characteristic purity and power. Its subject, therefore, is the
minimal consciousness one feels when pondering long on the
universe, minimal because the thinker is interned in his own
abstractions, a scenario without dialogue or person—doomed!
It is this situation which feels like the void and the inchoate
and is Becket's primal scene.
     This theatre is a form of poetry in the sense that its
atmosphere is its theme. The subject is the soul waiting in
anguish for the universe to declare itself.
     One can not, therefore, attribute its spiritual desola-
tion to the indifference of an *actual* universe, for we live

always in the particularity of nature where satisfaction does not depend on whether the universe cares. No, the desolation is the bleakness encountered in the outer reaches of abstraction. We shudder in terror not because the universe is indifferent but because the scenario is depersonalized. Death would be kinder.

We are not, then, in the presence of a new consciousness or a higher truth but of overpowering depersonalizing forces objectified and sealed off, experienced as void and inchoate.

We use so little of our imagination that when we create the unexpected, it looks as if we have transcended even ourselves.

Left alone, the imagination confounds more than it clarifies. This shows that it was not meant to be utilitarian and belongs to a different faculty, the aesthetic. Thoughts and emotions are attracted to a work of art, but when you talk about its meaning or the emotion it evokes, you are not talking about *its* essential character.

When the imagination begins to play analogies with the abstractions, destiny and art, an axiom appears: "The first given is destiny; everything thereafter is art."

This is how errors are made, systems are built, and pundits lull.

The moment the creative imagination stops functioning, the value of life is thrown into question; and then its meaning.

What are we to conclude from this?

Now that philosophers have entered the modern world and turned their attention to utilitarian subjects, the field has been left to the poets.

Does our ancient interest mean that there is some correspondence between our quest for form and the impulse to discover the nature of being?

Magister qua magister, something very different from a judge. Anybody can be a magister. All he has to do is to assume the robe and utter maxims.

Would a man be spouting maxims if he were not wearing the robe?

Anonymous does not make maxims.

Myths look as if they were struggling with some distant insight but are not quite able to get it into focus and so they tell a story instead. Yet with so little to go on, the speculations on their cosmic meaning would fill the British Museum. Obviously the myth's real hero is theory.

Art has one motivation which brings it close to games and occupations: to revamp life and bring it under control.

Normally our organs serve each other so precisely that all we are aware of, if we make a conscious effort, is a single ectoplastic presence, and in the rear, dimly on a lower threshold, the eyes and mind working, and the erect spine, their support. Living in Mexico, however, one soon discovers that all this rests on a large bowel, of mealy substance, queasy, stirring, loose, with a bottom that could drop out any minute and the legs buckle under like rubber if its cyclop is aroused. When that nether ur-giant stirs, the scribe atop the brain stem stops at once and waits for directions.

Old ideas are as hard as garbage to dispose of once and for all.

Theory acts as if its only motive was to discover truth and serve man faithfully and be his trained seal. Instead, it turns him into one.

Where there is intuition, there is theory trying to bribe it with credentials to stay within familiar bounds and become an honest woman.

Person, a word derived from *persona*, a face mask used by actors; hence a character—as if it were man's character to conceal his real self and Shakespeare's "All the world's a stage" were literally true, in the sense perhaps that the mind, by acquiring information, forming prescribed habits, and following protocols in the everyday world sets up a cover for the hard-core self, the timid soul which feels safe and will venture out with its insight only behind the protection of a mask.

But the humanist will never buy that.

The poet starts with a representation, hears and observes himself doing it, then observes his response and responds to that, and thus bit by bit develops his theme.

The psychology is the same as in relationships. There too one starts with a representation—viz., that one's wife is hostile—responds with anger to that as if it were really so, thereby making the wife actually hostile if she was not so before. The representation now stands confirmed and reinforced. Henceforth they are locked into a closed system in which they both comport themselves as if the representation were the real issue between them, as it is in poetry.

We borrow so much from representations in books, in the media, and from all those who know more than we, that no one is sure any longer what is authentically his own. Thus, artists search the arts and men flock to encounter groups as to an Age of Innocence to discover what is real and human in themselves. The remedy, unfortunately, can only be another representation, for representation is implanted in the mind as its very quality.

In love it is that which is moving and beautiful, not the sensory experience. The representation, in fact, is necessary to the feeling, and is enough by itself to induce it.

Like an ancient god it has a dual face: one side makes us human and benign, the other impersonal. Therein lies the poet's special poignancy.

He who reveals the consequences of society on himself leaps across the intervening distance.

If the purpose of *Die Kunst der Fuge* had been to draw attention to the grandeur of its composer, it would not have been grand but grandiose, despite its grand design.

On the stage is an actor trying to be someone other than he is.

On the movie screen is a photograph of an actor trying to be someone other than he is.

It is easier for the photograph to be that other person. It has the advantage of being incorporeal.

Understatement is no more virtuous than overstatement. It should be left to the banker. He *has* to be conservative.

In the everyday world what passes for change in a human being is adaptation or just a changing of persona, but the ceaseless obsession with progress calls this "growth." The fact is that inner change, if it takes place at all, could only occur in existential contemplation, where there are no roles and persona, and the inner self lies in the dark, a shapeless flux, feeling both a limitless, awful power and a pitiful weakness, terrified of change, ceaselessly seeking stability and form. But you'd never know it from the mad equation, Change is Progress.

American idea: if God is anything like man, He must have tender feelings towards us, we are so minute, so vulnerable, yet so gutsy and probing.

"Le tableau est fini quand il a éffacé l'idée."
(Braque, *Notebooks*, 1917-1947)
Precisely. And along comes the poet turned art-critic, doing his darndest to *create* an idea for it, putting it back into the state from which the artist liberated it. Not very sensible, but a good show. Artists are not going to object, of course. Why should they bite the hand that gives them class and culture and sells pictures? Besides, it's interesting for non-painterly reasons to join the spectators and listen in on what non-painters make of their work.

As soon as a book is published, the curtain goes up and a total stranger, the literary critic, acting like the master of ceremonies, strides out on the stage and announces,
"All right, genius, step aside and let the intellectuals take over now." There seem to be no other stage directions.
The book now has passed into another phase. Men are busy, making a place for it in the culture, writing history from it, assuming that the writer's style was a response to social forces or a strategem for moving the art of writing ahead. This is how the work then is justified and writers become chess pieces.

Academicians have been blamed for so much that they have joined their attackers. They have become regular fellows, relevant, salty, avant garde. But if they are not really turned on by poetry, they have no defence against mistaking facility for the real thing.

The new Prometheus is not chained to a rocky promontory but to a hallucination that there is nothing real, that the universe is limitless and bare, held together by rigor, the imagination random and automatic . . . above all, unpeopled.

In short, the media have taken the place of personal experience, and the vulture eating his bowels is depersonalization.

Nevertheless, Prometheus remains incorrigibly romantic. The proof is that he has succeeded in making this landscape look fascinating.

Why would anybody in his right mind want to show how arid and meaningless existence is? For hubris, that's why! to prove that he can look at the "real" nature of things without flinching or having to humanize it.

The child of media histrionics, still romantic and puritan, has perhaps no other place to go.

How the intellectuals truckle up to Black Comedy and suck!

George Oppen and I have been friends for over sixty years although we did not meet or correspond with each other until 1971. This is understandable only if you know George. The way it happened was that we sat around his kitchen table in San Francisco and talked and ate cheese and bread, and the more we talked and the more I looked into his steady eyes, the deeper down we got to something solid and brotherly between us, older than he or I. That is how we became old, old friends in one night.

George is a tough old bird. He's the only man I know who can get away with the curious notion that feelings don't have to be expressed in poetry; they can be assumed from the situation. He gets away with it because he's patient and his eye will not let itself be distracted from its object. George has a great eye, precise and irreducible. If you sit still and look hard enough, you can see what it sees: it feels like the gnarled bark of an oak tree. The tree is there too. You can put your weight against it. It won't give.

It is no longer clear why Stravinsky's ballets are sad. Is it because they are stylized, the life in them only make-believe, or because this was as close to life as Stravinsky could get without being sentimental and derivative? Ergo, the mock hero, absented to the remote parameters of a charmed circle while the tiger of reality lurked outside and sometimes raged.

With the years it has become harder to feel its enchantment. One can't identify with characters who can never be larger than pantomime and who live as if life were a small memory.

Stravinsky the man who understands the world is preferable. In his later years he apparently thought so too, for he composed *The Rake's Progress*, but he would have objected to applying literary considerations on the ground that music is closer to mathematics than to literature.

Men who are not in danger during a war remain ideological. That's why wars drag on.

When the Administration takes a moral tone, run for the hills. You will not be able to resist the general expectation that you lay down your life for words, like *supreme importance.*

The conscience is unaware that human nature does

not behave like words, with rhetorical magnitude.

Friends are not made; they are recognized.

No man wants to be someone else; he only wants what someone else possesses. This tenacity is too basic to be conscious.

The Good Soldier Schweik, a relentless reporter, intent on finding out how badly the country is hemorrhaging inside, sticks a microphone at Senator Eagleton's face after it came out that he had withheld information about a mental breakdown and had blown his chances for the vice-presidential nomination: "How do you feel now, Senator?"

Ideals are absolutes. If you fall in love with them, you have to exaggerate and become a romantic autocrat. That's what happened to the liberal.

The function of the arts under Communism is to improve its rhetoric and enable its theory to look ultimate.

People's natural skepticism towards larger-than-life abstractions is easily washed out. All it takes is for an established writer to universalize his state of consciousness. It will be regarded as a form of deeper and higher understanding.

Bring in the anti-critics to clear the categories out of our way!

Men are willing to risk their lives in a war and endure the worst for the same reason that they are our friends, because they are trusting and good natured.

The old radical cartoonists like Art Young and William Gropper had the right idea. They knew who the real enemy was . . . not men but ideas. They knew, for example, that for an idea like "The credibility of the U.S. as a stabilizing force in the world must never be allowed to come into question," whole countries can be butchered. That's why I say those old timers had the right idea when they drew public figures as embodiments of ideas and caricatured them as repulsive monsters, for the consequences of such ideas *are* loathsome and monstrous and it was a public service to drag them out from behind their lofty tone for everybody to see.

If the Church stopped canonizing, the implication would be that it had all been a mistake or that it no longer had the capacity to recognize a saint when it saw one. Thanks to this, the Croats finally got a saint of their own, despite the skeptical times, Nicola Tavelic, who had been burned to death six hundred years before by Moslems in Jerusalem.

They say that if industrial combustion continues at the present rate of growth, by the year 2000 there will be so much carbon dioxide in the air that the atmosphere will become a hot greenhouse and the Arctic Ice Cap will melt and slump into the sea, raising a tidal wave ten stories high which will wipe out most of mankind.
Yeh, if, if, if.

140

Some knucklehead is always turning his eyes up to heaven and bemoaning the conflict between the artist and society.

God forbid society should dance to the tune of its artists.

This conflict is exactly what the artist needs to bring out his full resources and individuality.

The intellect and the imagination seem always ready for new ventures, but to feelings a limit has been set by morality with its aversions, which we pretend are matters of taste because the intellect does not take morality altogether seriously.

Nature is kind. When a toothache is over, it's over. All we remember is the language for it.

When the unknowable, and the imagination on which it rides, turns towards us, it has the face of a monument from ancient times when men could contemplate.

Even religion has ceased being contemplative.

Only the poets and a few romantic theologians are left.

Money is real. I am no more greedy for it than for blood or earth.

"I've been telling you all the good things that have happened to me," said my friend, after a long separation, beaming. "What about you?"

So I told him matter of factly that I was having another book published in the fall.

His smile froze. The light left his eyes.

He remembered with a heavy heart how he had been a better father than a son; but if he had it to do over, it would be the same.

After he retired, the most joyous moment in his life came to him. It was when he was driving his wife down to work one morning, bumper to bumper, two abreast, in a stream of cars whose end could not be seen, in each a tense face knotted like a squirrel's at the mouth and eyes, where the business of the day had already come together as intersecting vectors and was being transacted, and he thought, "Nobody can ever fire me now. Never!"

Once the intangible becomes tangible enough to be measured, it becomes ordinary and has a short interest span.

If it is true that we value originality more than they did in the ancient world, one reason for it may be that they had no need for it yet. They had not yet become exposed to depersonalizing forces or bored with the familiar.

Some words have a genius for being useful. Like the word, *chance*. If you merely speculate about the meaning of chance, it remains philosophical and retains some of the original inscrutability which the word was invented to dispose of. But to the social scientists the word is as real as a nail. Not only have they worked out its theory and mathematics but they have been poring over it for some time, sleeves rolled up, planning the parameters of the twenty-first century.

THE POET

I

POETRY

Its nature is to look
                        both absolute and mortal,
as if a boy had passed through
or the imprint of his foot
                        had been preserved
unchanged under the ash of Herculaneum.

II

IMAGE

Fly low
        out of the saltpit
my vernacular
           thrush

III

When he sat down to his desk
                         in the morning
there was a voice
                    weeping
from the personal
                    which could not bear its frailty
and longed for alleviation
in some lovely figure or perception.

Sometimes it spoke
                    as if it knew it was going to be published:
"I will never sacrifice man for art."

It needed no one
and was neither modest nor superior,
just sure and straight.
When he heard it, he knew he had a good thing
and wrote it down,
at first plain
                and then as high character,
as if he were discovering his nature.

But the commitment had already been made
to honesty and clarity.
Why then did he have to go through
                              all that strangeness?

IV

The simile flew
                    out of chance,
belly aglow,
                    but when he looked in
for his breath,
                    the light expired
as from a firefly.
Yet on the reader's earth
this was a pyramid of Cheops.

                    O eternal
is its element!

V

THE EXECUTION

poet opens a box:
                    empty!
Where is the god?
                    in syntax . . .
on linguistic wires . . .
                         out of sight!

And longing?
          where's the god of that?
It has been Englished.
                    It bleeds no more.

VI

As the body of mystery
                          to a field of force
is the symbol.

For approaching a mystery
                          and for transcending,
which is the origin of human nature
and where all value is
                          as beauty is in the eye,
there is a ceremony.

So we must get on with the poem.

VII

NINE NATURES OF METAPHOR

It liberates its referent
from matter.

It is its own state,
incommunicado absolute.

The author writes:
"There is a destiny in form
which led here."

But its origin has been deleted
like the circle's
which entered geometry
and became a line.

It governs by high portents
promissory in its language
and by illusion sits beyond understanding

and procreates on sight. Unchecked,
it could occupy the earth.

The moment it appears, it is a given
(like the concept
                    of atomic number).

It is without soul,
yet men follow it;

without matter,
yet not incredible;

and lies in an amnion
and approaches infinity.

Nevertheless, I will not drink to it.
I'll drink to iron,
                    I'll drink to Shem,

I'll drink to salamander,
but not to that.

O.K., a goddess.
But hold on to your balls.

VIII

The big birds
          look impervious.
The young child's image
of his father
          with imperishable head
goes down with him to the grave
and all the great unmoved ones
                    look long distances
but inside are small,
for sweetness from the knowledge of mortality
                              spurts
as from a spring
          and only when it runs dry
needs the bird
          austere, immovable
seeing beauty in it.

Only language is both sweet and enduring.

IX

FORTIFICATIONS

The light hair
                will guard the skin
and the inlets
                of the nose
and ass

while you,
                well-hidden glands,
wash out the eyes
                and teeth

and poetry
                for double protection
stands outside
                on call
like an Aesculapian dog
                to lick ulcers.

X

TUNE

Today I was pleased by the image
                    of the Japanese wrestler
legs apart
            hair tied in the back
looking like Turkey
                    astride the Anatolian fault

and a voice in me
                cried
"Let us go down to the river
                    and find Armenia

and listen again to that way of speaking in Vasari:
'It is related that Giorgione
                        in conversation
with certain sculptors
                    at the time
when Andrea del Verrocchio was engaged with his bronze horse . . . .' "

XI

"A statelier pyramis to her I'll rear
than Rhodope's of Memphis ever was."

Not in Tennessee
                    nor in ancient Egypt
but where time
                    and place shift
as when a dream draws to its exigent.
There you will see the real
                              Memphis radioactive
rising out of memory
                    with all its pyramises.

XII

THE CHINA POLICY

Of all the old times
　　　　　　　I'll take Chinese poetry.
A man could loll under a hemlock tree then
　　　　　　　　　　　　　and muse,
and nature be
　　　　　　as wood to carpenters,
a grouse ambling by,
　　　　　　　　a sparrow hopping . . .
nothing was of greater consequence . . .
　　　　　　　　　　　such sweetness flowing
as through a membrane through his limbs
　　　　　　　　　　the universe turned
into a poet's enclave,
　　　　　　　　the great society
where simplicity is character
　　　　　　　　and character the common tongue,
the representative of man.

In those corrupt, bitter times
　　　　　　　　　the most obscure clerk
could attain clarity
　　　　　　　from these poems,
and his nature,
and change into a superior man
　　　　　　　　　of exquisite modesty
by simply looking at a heron crossing a stream.

XIII

THE TRANSMUTATION INTO ENGLISH

"Let the young men come to the study of nature
and learn what is fixed
and what is transient.
Life is too short otherwise."
                              (Aristotle . . . more or less)

Once he sets about it, every man has a theory
no smaller than the universe
and an Ariel in it
who will carry an integer and a nul for him
to a star's power,
so let him beware of his agents,
for it is one thing to be Paracelsus and the first man
to make ether, and another to theorize
that every living thing has an archeus,
making one a beech tree,
                              one a mackerel,
and one a quartz,
and still another to understand nature.

And let them watch their examples,
for in England the example of quintessence
is *The Law Of England*
is the quintessence of reason.

They will try to sneak into heaven on that word,
especially the poets, who are likely to be found
under the robes of magister
or where philosophy looks from a rock
or in the eye,
                              the supreme governor,
or where conclusion lies in a name,
as in Alexander of Aphrodisias

or nesting in a phrase,
                              "the gravel of God,"
in the place where man feels
                              the final declaration

of mass and destiny,
               whereas "the onion of gods"
is a kind of goat
               kicking up its heels in the mind,

or looking at horses,
               Giorgione's horse
which started out as a plane
                    on a canvas,
and the bronze horse
                    which was made because
Andrea del Verrocchio liked to walk around it
and feel the various parts with his hand,
crying out that he felt things beyond understanding,
he would not settle for understanding,
his horse was the imagination,
and he was not satisfied with the horse either;

in other words, in the fifth element
if all matter is composed of three elements
and the fourth is comedy.

XIV

Who died here?
            Where's the body?

No place.
        That weeping
is the tone
          of poetic prose.

I could have sworn
                a pessimist
was buried there.

No.
    Just the word.
It comes off the tongue
in hard lacquer.

No roast beef then.

No. Only guava and quince.

Too bad. It is an indulgent country.

XV

ASSOCIATIONS WITH A VIEW FROM THE HOUSE

What can be compared to
                the living eye?
its East
        is flowering
honeysuckle
           and its North
dogwood bushes.

What can be compared
             to light
in which leaves darken
             after rain,
fierce green?
         like Rousseau's jungle:
any minute
        the tiger head
will poke through
           the foliage
peering
      at experience.

Who is like man
         sitting in the cell
of referents,
        whose eye
has never seen
        a jungle,
yet looks in?

It is the great eye,
         source of security.
Praised be thou,
        as the Jews say,
who have engraved clarity
and delivered us to the mind
           where you must
reign severe as quiddity of bone
            forever and ever
without bias or mercy,
without attrition or mystery.

XVI

The other day
              I was typing Aug. 7, 1972
and forgot to drop
              to lower case.
Instantly a communication
                    appeared
which circulates ordinarily
only among its own kind:
              AUG. ↷, L(↷".
It had the allure of the impenetrable.
                                In fact,
it didn't have to be understood at all,
even on whether it cared for human beings.
That was its greatest charm.
                    In short, it was grounded
on the unconditional,
              one of the attributes of beauty.

XVII

What rides the galaxies
                    on calculations,
is disinterested as air
                    and long as equanimity,
yet weeps unknowing
                    when it stops,
and shivers,
            withdrawing like the overbreeding
muskrat,
            downcast at itself?

XVIII

HIS DREAM

They are stoning images, mother,
                           breaking windows
in the American Embassy
                and shouting NO MORE MYSTIQUES!
This time it's the intellectuals.
                           They are pouring into the street.

If they come face to face
                           with the blue-eyed boy from Iowa
or the black man,
                what then?

XIX

So now he can't stand
              either a conservative or a liberal,
but a detail is enough
              to break his heart.

Item
"The clear glass hearse
              was pulled by two
immense black horses."

Item
"The corpse entered
              a grove of walnut trees."

XX

Because of envy
I am ashamed.
The malignant god has entered
my blood stream.
My limbs are twisted.

An iron rod
is jammed into my gut:
"This man's work is great."
I can think of nothing else.
There is no hope for me.
Because of fear.

O, I am sick!
My mouth is dry.
I possess nothing.
One look from the covetous god
has finished me.

Mercy, great god.
I have been shamed enough.
I will acknowledge you.
Let me get to my own work
with the necessary innocence.

XXI

A man
      is fiddling with his matchbox
while he talks,
exactly as I saw him
           thirty years ago.
I have his tweed coat on
           (I can feel the coarse fabric),
his domestic habits,
the abstract look in his eyes.

Now to break out
         of this straightjacket!

XXII

As soon as I know its compass
I can write the poem.

If my suspicions were more grandiose
and I had the bile of a prophet
or could space myself out on high
                                    metaphors
I could go long distances too.

XXIII

BEING NATURAL

How hard one has to labor at it.
There are explanations, of course,
and confessions,
but that is not what is meant.

The way is lost.
The character is gone.

XXIV

THE BLANK PAGE

What's the matter?
                    Have you nothing
to say about America?

Do you not dare be
                  grandiose?

XXV

Heavy hangs
        the age of occupation
over the romantic head.

Who will now be greater
            than the sabre-toothed tiger
and preserve the divine proportion
                of a game of chess?

Who will sit
        in his mind
and scan the planet
          as a small island?

Who will remember
          that when Osiris is at 12
on the dial
        and the invention of surveying, 6,
it's Egypt?

Who will be left
          to smell the pine and eucalyptus
and make a theme-head
            impersonate a god?

XXVII

LETTING THE SPIRIT OUT

The reader before the inner
                            space in a poem:
"Ah, my element!"
                    He takes a deep breath.
"If I forget again
                    I deserve to stew
in everlasting intellectual chores."

                        He forgot.

XXVII

THE METAPHOR

Another small
           universe of Adam
enters
    on the great page
and shines
      for a moment.

Hola!

XXVIII

THE VOW

Matter,
      with this look
I wed thee
        and become
thy very
       attribute.
I shall
    be thy faithful
spouse,
      true
to thy nature,
        for I love
thee
   more than Dürer
loved a seaweed.

Printed August 1975 in Santa Barbara & Ann Arbor
for the Black Sparrow Press by Noel Young
& Edwards Brothers Inc. Typography by
Graham Mackintosh. Design by Barbara Martin.
This edition is published in paper wrappers;
there are 200 hardcover copies numbered &
signed by the poet; & 26 lettered copies
handbound in boards by Earle Gray each with
an original holograph poem by Carl Rakosi.

Carl Rakosi was born in 1903 in Berlin, Germany. From 1904 to 1910 he lived with his grandparents in Baja, Hungary, his parents having been divorced. In 1910 he and an older brother, Lester, came to live with his father, Leopold Rakosi, and his stepmother, Rose Kulka. Leopold Rakosi was a watchmaker and had a jewelry store, first in Gary, Indiana, and then, until his death, in Kenosha, Wisconsin. Carl Rakosi attended the University of Wisconsin (B.A. in English and M.A. in psychology) and the University of Pennsylvania (Master of Social Work degree) and subsequently took clinical training in psychotherapy. Until his retirement in 1968 he worked as a social worker and psychotherapist in New York, Chicago, Boston, New Orleans, Houston, St. Louis, Cleveland, and finally Minneapolis, where he has lived since 1945. He is married to Leah Jaffe and has two children and four grandchildren.

His poems first appeared in *The Little Review* and in Ezra Pound's *The Exile* in the 1920s. In the early 1930s he was associated briefly with the Objectivists. His first book, *Two Poems*, appeared in 1933 (The Modern Editions Press). Then came *Selected Poems* (New Directions, 1941). However, by 1940 he had stopped writing entirely and did not resume until 1966. Both early and new work are in his volume, *Amulet* (New Directions, 1967). This was followed by *Ere-Voice* (New Directions, 1971).

He was Writer-in-Residence at the University of Wisconsin, 1969-70; on the faculty of the National Poetry Festival in 1973, and Visiting Poet at Michigan State University in 1974. In 1969 and 1972 he won awards from the National Endowment for the Arts.